Mastering C Pointers

Mastering C Pointers

Tools for Programming Power

Robert J. Traister

Academic Press, Inc.
Harcourt Brace Jovanovich, Publishers
San Diego New York Boston
London Sydney Tokyo Toronto

This book is printed on acid-free paper. ∞

Academic Press, Inc.
San Diego, California 92101

United Kingdom Edition published by
Academic Press Limited
24–28 Oval Road, London NW1 7DX

Library of Congress Cataloging-in-Publication Data

Traister, Robert J.
Mastering C pointers : tools for programming power / Robert J. Traister.
p. cm.
ISBN 0-12-697408-X (alk. paper)
1. C (Computer program language) I. Title.
QA76.73.C15T697 1990
005.26'2--dc20 89-18384
CIP

Printed in the United States of America
90 91 92 93 9 8 7 6 5 4 3 2 1

Dedicated to the memory of
Joseph Frank Silek, Sr.

Contents

Preface

C language has been called "the best language for microcomputers" by many experts in the field. This, of course, is opinion, but it is an undisputed fact that the C programming language is the hottest language going today. Little more than an exotic curiosity cloaked in mystery 10 or 15 years ago, it is now the major programming tool of the great majority of commercial software producers. As important, C language has made its way boldly (and often quite bluntly) into the realm of the noncommercial or hobby programmer. I say "as important" because it is from this area that tomorrow's crack programmers will emerge.

When I wrote my first book on C language nearly a decade ago, C was quite obscure. On a promotional tour to one of our western states during the early 1980s, I was somewhat amazed to learn that my presence increased that state's C programmer population by 33%. I was only the fourth known C programmer in that state.

Yes, C and microcomputers have enjoyed a close, profitable relationship. However, C has a notorious reputation of being extremely difficult to learn. A lot of this reputation is undeserved and probably dates back to a time when few (if any) educational materials were available for this language. C has a relatively small set of functions and statements which is conducive to a quick study. On the other hand, C enjoys a very weird syntax, which is a good part of its "difficult" reputation.

The most difficult aspect of the C programming language lies in its rather avant-garde use of pointers. Now, if you are entering C from an assembly language environment, manipulating and programming with pointers may not cause a lot of difficulty. However, if you come form a BASIC language environment, then there is every likelihood that you don't even know what a pointer is.

As one who programs daily in C, who teaches the C programming language, and who conducts seminars and workshops about learning this language, I have found that pointer operations fall into a category that could best be labeled "FEAR." And it is not only the novice who fears pointers and their operations. Relatively seasoned programmers, some of whom have been "playing" with C language for a year or more, will often do everything possible to avoid the use of pointers.

Fact: If you do not fully understand pointers and how they may be used, then you simply don't know how to program in C, period.

Certainly, some highly interesting and even useful programs may be written in C without resorting to declared pointer operations. However, the great majority of these programs could be made more efficient and could be written with quite a bit less effort if the programmer only understood C language pointers. Pointer operations encompass one of the most powerful aspects of the C programming language . . . and one of the most interesting! You must know this area of the language at least as well as you know any other area.

This book was written for one reason: To take the mystery out of C language pointers by explaining exactly what they are through easy-to-understand phrasing and via many, many simple program examples. If you are a beginning C language programmer, then welcome. This text should provide you with the basic understanding about the "muscle" side of C. Once this basic knowledge has been imparted, you should find it much easier to move on and through the other areas of this fascinating programming language. If you are an experienced programmer, you are also welcome. I believe that you will find the discussions throughout this text to be of value in enhancing your current knowledge of the C programming language.

I assure you that if every chapter in this text is read in its entirety and each program example studied until you are sure of its workings, then by book's end, C language pointers will no longer be a mystery to you. You will be able to boldly go where you have never gone before, confident that your understanding of C pointers will enable you to go full throttle without the handicap of misunderstanding.

As a further introduction to the start of this learning experience, let me state emphatically that the concept of pointers is a very simple one. Manipulating pointers and using them to great advantage is merely a matter of throwing off the shroud of mystery and exposing this special variable for what it truly is. I believe you will be surprised at what a small stumbling block the C language pointer has been. You will also be amazed at the new world of programming that this aspect of the C programming language offers you. The first step in mastering the C programming language lies in mastering the C language pointer. It is hoped that you will consider Chapter 1 of this text as step number 1 on this journey to C language mastery.

Robert J. Traister

Chapter 1

C Language and Pointers—A Personal Background

The C programming language, since its introduction in the very early 1970s, has progressed from the "personal" language of an elite group of programmers at Bell Laboratories to a somewhat exotic language of daring professional programmers and finally to the language of an ever-growing diversified number of "average" programmers. This latter group consists of you and me, of professional programmers, of brand-new novices, and of those who work for the major software houses. C, then, has become an almost universal language. It has been described by many as the best language for microcomputers and by others as the best all-around language ever. These opinions are certainly arguable and argued, but one fact is certain: C is an extremely popular object-oriented programming language that has made inroads into every fiber of the computer programming world.

The current popularity of C and the wealth of books, compilers, interpreters, and other forms of documentation are a far, far cry from the situation in the early 1980s. At that time, C was only a decade old, Kernighan and Ritchie were about the only ones who had dared to write about C, and compilers were almost as scarce as documentation. In 1981, C was a mysterious language, its rites practiced by only a small group I have often referred to as a "priesthood." And to those of us who were intent on learning this new language, this priesthood would often as not hand down the edict of "C is not for mortal man!!!"

Indeed, my first encounters with the C programming language could only be described as tragic. When I was finally able to latch onto a C compiler that cost less than $600, I was astounded by the fact that it simply didn't work. No, I didn't receive a piece of defective media as would be the case with a damaged disk or improper copy; I got a compiler that simply didn't work. After weeks of calling the software company (which shall remain nameless) that supplied it, I got another version. Guess what? This one didn't work, either. Finally on the third try, the compiler worked . . . after a fashion. It still had an incredible number of bugs, supported only a subset of the original C programming language, and was a complete abomination.

With this Frankensteinian C compiler, I was finally able to compile and run my first C program, the famous K&R (Kernighan and Ritchie) "hello, world." While this was an exciting event for me personally, the fact that 3 months had elapsed since I had received the first compiler seemed to dictate that something else was needed. Even the third version of this compiler (the one that worked . . . sort of) made it almost impossible to put to practice the little I had learned from K&R's "The C Programming Language." Most of their teachings were simply not supported.

It was at this point that I vowed to give up on C completely. Indeed, I didn't try C again for almost 8 months. However, a gratis copy of the now famous Lattice C Compiler arrived in my office one day. When I finally got around to using it, I found that the scant few things I knew about C language were perfectly workable under this excellent compiler, and I progressed at a somewhat faster pace. Still, there were many things missing that I had become accustomed to as a BASIC programmer. Why were there no functions to clear the screen? Hey! They could at least have supplied a square-root function. I would even have settled for a peek/poke routine that would allow me to address all of my IBM PC's memory.

Well, those things were yet to come, and they eventually did. Fortunately for me, the expanded-function set did not arrive before I had figured out how to write many of the most needed math and screen utility functions on my own, a learning experience that was invaluable. In those days, a C compiler that supported floating-point math operations as opposed to integers-only was considered a luxury item. Today, a C compiler that doesn't include the latest ANSI (American National Standards Institute) standard set of functions with its elaborate assortment of baubles, whistles, and bells is something to (rightfully) scorn.

The documentation field has grown with the C programming language over the last decade. In 1980, K&R's "The C Programming Language" was the only published source on the C programming language. This excellent work, by the authors' own admission, was not an introductory programming manual. It seemed so technical and foreign to me at the time that it's a wonder that I ever persisted. It was only after I had struggled for a year or more making every mistake possible in C that I had learned enough on my own to be able to fully appreciate the terse, dry wording of this book, and to learn from it. Even today, I keep it nearby as a familiar reference source.

Today, the market abounds with C language books . . . books for all skill levels and pursuits. If you're a BASIC programmer, then there is specialized help for you in one of many books. If you know C but want to know more, the intermediate-level books are also in abundance. There are as many more aimed at higher level users. Yes, things have sure changed since the early 1980s as far as learning the C programming language is concerned.

Except in one area! The subject of C language pointers and pointer operations is still a partially unexplored curriculum. Sure, most forms of books and other documentation do offer a chapter on C pointers, but these are usually very incomplete. This is quite understandable, because C pointers require at least an entire book for a worthwhile explanation. Several large volumes could easily be filled in fully explaining the meaning, purpose, operation, and versatility of the pointer.

C pointer operations constitute one of the greatest stumbling blocks for persons learning the language. Most texts that discuss C pointers only skim the surface. It would seem that those authors who know a lot about pointers often assume that their readership does also. Those who know a lot about the other aspects of the language half-heartedly broach the subject just to round out the text contents. Both ways, not enough "raw" material is presented. The result is a growing number of persons who call themselves C programmers but who really don't understand the full extent of the power C pointers offer. Of course, "power" programming is an overused phrase. A good, basic knowledge of C language pointers allows the programmer a relaxed and almost artistic method of handling tasks. You can certainly program in C without resorting to declared pointers, but you can't program as expressively nor as efficiently as you can with pointers.

As is always the case, progress in C language compilers has lessened the chore of the programmer. Prototyping has finally come about, and this provides a relatively high degree of "protection" regarding the passing of arguments to functions. Without prototyping, data type requirements are more exacting. For instance, passing an int variable or constant to a function that requires a double type will result in "garbage" returns using older C compilers. With prototyping, the math functions are more versatile, since arguments of the incorrect data type are coerced (cast) to correct types where possible.

All of this is excellent from a user standpoint but probably not so useful to the student trying to grasp the "concept" of this very efficient, very expressive language. This outlook may be starting to sound like the proverbial "good ol' days" approach, wherein someone espouses the virtues of the one-room school, the outhouse, and the horse and buggy. This is not my intention at all! Prototyping is a powerful new tool to C programming, but it should be used to enhance program efficiency, not to make up for bad programming methods. Bad programming technique will eventually catch up with you no matter how many safeguards are built into a C compiler.

The only aim of this text is to reveal the C language pointer. It's not really that much different from any other type of variable. For the most part, all program examples will be short, sweet, and plentiful. Prototyping will not be used, as we will be sticking solely to the very basics of the language. Once these are grasped, the fancy "whistles and tin horns" built into today's compilers will become even more valuable and will enhance each program you write.

You are encouraged to simply "play" with some of the ideas that will be presented in this text, for it is through such play that new concepts and techniques may be explored. More realistically, recreational programming will yield a tremendous amount of programming mistakes that can be worked out at the reader's leisure and will probably never be forgotten. The "impossible-to-correct" error that is finally overcome is worth more from a tutorial standpoint than all of the documentation you are ever likely to read about the same program operation.

The model compiler used for discussions in this text is the Borland Turbo C compiler, Version 2.0. Borland came up with a winner in this package that cost less than one-third of the going price for the most popular C compilers out at the time of its release. Additionally, Turbo C Version 1.0 compiled faster, produced smaller code, and executed faster than any of the "big three" compilers on the market at the time. Since the introduction of Turbo C, these other C language compiler companies have answered the Borland challenge with faster, better, and cheaper compilers. The C language community has benefited greatly from this competition, and it is no longer necessary (in fact, it would be considered ridiculous) to pay $450, $600, $725, or more for a professional C compiler.

Programs in this text, for the most part, are written to be compiled using the small-memory-model option of Turbo C. This is the model that will produce the most efficient code, although several examples prefer or demand the large-memory model. Both of these and several other variations are included with the basic Turbo C package.

The model computer for researching this text was an IBM PC-XT with 640K memory, 40 megabyte hard disk, and a monochrome monitor. This is certainly representative of a minimum MS-DOS setup. All programs were executed on this system, but original programming was handled on a Wyse 386 system with all of the frills one might expect. This might be representative of a "high-end" user. The author had the convenience and speed of the 386 system for original authoring, but all program examples and discussions surround execution on the low-end system.

The discussions in this book assume the reader has more than a conversational knowledge of C programming. This is not a tutorial on the entire language. It can be accurately stated that the text is aimed at advanced beginners to intermediate-level programmers. These are individuals who feel relatively comfortable writing C programs but who feel that they have some distance to travel when it comes to the topic of pointers.

It is quite possible, even likely, that many readers will have developed an erroneous concept of pointers and pointer operations. I speak from experience in this area. Because of the gloss-over approach taken by many forms of C documentation, such false impressions are easy to come by.

This text is written from a personal standpoint that may be best described as "I wish someone had told me this years ago when I was pulling my hair out trying to learn this aspect of the language." If I have any notable talent, it lies in never forgetting just how ignorant I once was. As I write these words, I think back to the years 1981 and 1982. I not only remember but still "feel" the frustration of trying to learn C by the "let's try everything until something works" method. Remember, there were no primers for C in those days. There was no one available anywhere (it seemed) to answer the most rudimentary questions. I finally came across a C programmer through a newspaper ad in a major city who agreed to write some simple programs involving C language file-keeping routines that I could use on a self-tutorial basis. What sounded like a reasonable rate of "sixteen" dollars per hour turned out to be "SIXTY!!" dollars per hour. ("Gee Bob, you must have misunderstood me, I said *sixty* dollars per hour.") In any event, I received about an hour's worth of the most rudimentary C programs, received a bill for 10 hours, and paid $600.00 for programs I can now write in total within the span of 20 minutes. Sure, I was ripped off . . . but I learned from those programs. Maybe it was worth six *thousand* dollars! Today, you can learn one hundred times as much for less than twenty dollars at your local bookstore.

This tale of woe and misery describes my roots in the C programming language. However, these experiences have been invaluable to me from the standpoint of remembering my complete ignorance at that time and, most important, what I learned to overcome that state of affairs. Hopefully these experiences will be of benefit to you, the reader, as I attempt to impart some of the things I learned in these pages.

Chapter 2

A First Step to Learning Pointers

In C language, a pointer is a special variable that holds a memory address . . . and that's all it is! Pointers may be treated as standard variables in many ways, but the adjective "special" also means that they cannot be treated like standard variables in other operations. In some ways they can be used in high-powered constructs like no other standard variable. Therefore, there are several familiar aspects that can be seen in C pointers and several that will be unfamiliar to those programmers who are not accustomed to using pointers. Careless (although technically correct) use of pointers can easily result in a hodgepodge program that is nearly impossible to understand because of the misdirection.

It is highly advantageous to review some C programming basics, especially in regard to addressing and memory allocation, before moving headlong into the topic of pointers. Pointer operations cannot be fully understood until the storage methods used in C language are clearly fixed in the programmer's mind. These storage methods and rules are handled by the compiler and are relatively invisible to the programmer by observing only what "seems" to be taking place. It is quite easy to form misconceptions, and these untruths and half-truths multiply into total learning chaos through the faulty use of pointers.

Let's begin the discussion by using the following simple C program as an example:

```
main()
{
        int x;

        x = 10;

        printf("%d\n", x);

}
```

Here, `x` is declared a standard (auto) variable of type `int`. It is assigned a value of 10, and its contents are displayed on the screen using **printf().** Nothing could be simpler. However, to fully understand pointer operations and to have a far better understanding of the "invisible" processes that take place within a computer program, it is necessary to dissect each operation carried out under **main().**

What happens when the variable is declared? The answer is that space is set aside at a location in memory to allow storage of a 2-byte value necessary to store numbers within the standard integer range. This 2-byte storage allocation is common for most MS-DOS machines running the most popular C compilers.

These 2 bytes are allocated somewhere in memory when the C program is executed. The exact whereabouts of this memory location are unimportant to the operation of this particular program. Now, the assignment line tells the computer to store a value of 10 in the 2 bytes reserved exclusively for variable `x`. This is stored as a 2-byte integer. The first byte will be equal to 10, while the second byte will equal zero. This is the 2-byte coding for a value of 10. Other combinations allow the 2 bytes to represent a positive value (unsigned) of up to 65,535 or positive/negative values of +32,767, or −32,768.

When the **printf()** function is executed, the value in x is displayed on the screen as an integer. Again, very simple. But it was desirable to go through each step of the program's operation, especially in regard to how memory is set aside for storage. This will become more and more important as the field of pointers is entered.

To repeat an earlier step in the program, the declaration of x as a variable of type int causes 2 bytes of "private" storage space to be set aside exclusively for this variable. We can find out exactly where this storage space is located in memory by using the ampersand operator (&) (also known as the "address-of" operator) as in:

```
main()
{

        int x;

        x = 10;

        printf("%u\n", &x);

}
```

Preceding the variable name (x) with the ampersand causes the memory location, also called the "starting address," of the variable to be returned instead of the value of the integer coded into this memory location. This gets into what is generally termed "lvalue" (left value) and "rvalue" (right value) designations. One is the memory address of the variable. The other is the quantity contained at the address. The &x designation is a pointer to the address of storage set aside for variable x. &x will always point to the address of storage that was automatically set aside to hold the contents of variable x. We can't change this memory address. It is fixed.

Note that the %u conversion specification is used in the format string argument to **printf()**, which displays the memory address as an unsigned integer. This is necessary, as the address is probably at the high end of the 64K segment used by most small-memory model C compilers. The actual address returned by `&x` can vary and is dependent on machine configurations, operating systems, and memory usage. Regardless of the value returned by `&x`, this is the memory location that has been reserved for the exclusive storage of values assigned to variable `x`.

Using the Turbo C compiler in the small-memory-model configuration on the test hardware used for researching this book, the above program will return a value of 65514. This means that bytes 65514 and 65515 within the 64K segment of memory were set aside exclusively for storing the integer values assigned to variable `x`. Referring to the first program example where `x` was assigned a value of 10, peeking into memory locations 65514 and 65515 would yield values of 10 and 0, respectively. Remember that, in this example, an int variable is allocated 2 bytes of storage. This 2-byte coding (10 and 0) yields a true value of 10 decimal. If the value assigned to variable `x` were changed to 1990, then the 2-byte coding would be 198 and 7, respectively. That is, the first byte assigned to variable `x` is equal to 198 while the second byte is equal to 7. This is the 2-byte coding for a decimal value of 1990.

The point to remember at this stage in the discussion is that `x` is a declared variable of type `int` and that `&x` is really a *constant* (at least it is during any single run of the C program under discussion). It cannot be changed as it is directly tied with variable `x` and is equal to the start of the address location set aside for the exclusive storage of assignments to `x`. In other words, we cannot reassign `&x` some other value. By definition and design, it is always equal to the start of memory assigned to `x`. Obviously an expression of:

```
&x = 99;
```

is completely illegal. `&x` can do only one thing. It returns the constant that names the address of storage for variable `x`. This is a very important point whose weight will be realized as we move on to further discussions. For a correct and useful understanding of pointer operations, it is necessary to know that there are two distinct values associated with all variables. (*Note:* Register variables are an exception and do not hold closely to the direction of this discussion.) The one we are most familiar with is the object value or the value that is assigned by the programmer as in:

```
x = 10;
```

In this example, the object value is 10 or the value that is contained at the memory locations specifically set aside for variable `x`. The second value associated with all variables is the memory address. This is the numeric location in memory where storage is set aside for the variable. The designation `&x` should not be thought of as an extension of the variable `x`. It should be considered a constant. Unlike a variable, its object cannot be reassigned. It is fixed. The unary ampersand operator (`&`) when used with a variable causes its address to be returned.

Referring to an earlier definition of a pointer (a special variable that contains a memory address and nothing else), `&x` would seem to qualify. Again, its value (in regard to memory location) is fixed. The `&x` designation can be used as the argument to a function that is looking for a pointer argument, and it does point to a place in memory. But this is only one expression of a pointer in C. Such a designation is not the type of pointer that is often referred to in C operations. We could cloud things further by referring to it as a "fixed" pointer, as it is fixed inextricably to the memory location of variable `x`. This will be explained in more detail a bit later.

Newcomers to the C programming language, especially BASIC programmers, are often cautioned about the dangers of unassigned variables. In the latter language, all numeric variables start out with initial values of zero. String values begin life with values of NULL. In C, the situation is completely different. When an auto variable is declared, only one basic operation takes place. Memory space is set aside exclusively for each declared variable. The bytes at these memory locations are not cleared or reset to zero as is the case with the BASIC language. Whatever bytes happened to be present at the memory location where storage is set aside remain in full force. Therefore, when, for instance, our `int x` variable was declared in an earlier program, the contents of the byte at memory location 65514 could be any value from 0 to 255. The same is true of the second byte at memory location 65515. If the programmer should mistakenly assume that the starting value of variable `x` is zero, then all sorts of problems can occur. The initial value of a declared variable, such as `int x`, has as much chance of being equal to zero as to any other number within the legal integer range. This is important to remember when dealing with declared pointers, because they can point to any memory location when they are first declared. All a pointer can do is contain or return an address in memory. What you do with or at this memory address is up to you, the programmer.

When a standard type of variable is declared, it must be remembered that the storage space that is automatically set aside for it can be considered "safe" storage. Different portions of computer memory are reserved for different things when a program is loaded and run. Some of these areas deal with program management and interface with the operating system. This area is the framework that allows the program to be properly executed. Storage for variables is not allocated in this area, because to do so would interrupt the framework and result in a crash. Therefore, a certain area of memory is set aside exclusively for variable storage. When dealing with declared pointers, we will learn that these latter variables are not restricted to safe areas like standard variables and can move anywhere in memory. This can result in execution catastrophe if the programmer is not on the ball.

The "Little Man" Approach

The ideal programming book, according to the publishers who sign authors to write them, is "of a high enough technical level to appeal to the professional programmer but which will also be useful to the novice trying to get a foothold on the subject." As one who is signed to write these books, I consider such a request on a par with designing a "full-fledged competition automobile that can out-accelerate any other race car and yet still gets 43 miles to the gallon for those persons who want an economy car." The two are not simultaneously possible. However, one must still make an attempt to offer technical materials in an environment that can include a broad range of readers.

As one who has learned several, diverse computer languages, I personally prefer to be treated like a complete novice and to read materials aimed at the beginner. In other words, I would rather a book be aimed at a readership just below my current technical expertise level than at one slightly advanced to the position I presently hold. I became very disgusted in my first attempts to learn LISP, because I had to search my interpreter manual and my technical books for several hours before I finally found the needed function to write to the screen. To my way of thinking, this should have been one of the first subjects discussed, because it allows readers to do a bit of experimenting on their own. Because of this personal preference of how I like to be taught, the "little man" portion of the next few chapters will be handled in a similar manner. This style is intended to get the reader quickly up to a higher level in using C pointers and *not* to talk down on the populace from some lofty tower. Thus enters the "little man" and his knapsack!

Taking up our discussion to this point, the single variable, `int x`, is likened to a little man with a knapsack on his back. In this knapsack, he has two compartments, each capable of holding a byte of information. He lives in a neighborhood that contains hundreds of different houses. Some are vacant, while others are home to more little men; sometimes there is only one to a household, sometimes more. These other neighbors also have knapsacks, some larger and some smaller than our first little man. For instance, the man that represents a long integer has a larger knapsack that contains four separate compartments, each holding a byte of information. The largest knapsack is owned by Mr. Double and has eight compartments for holding a double-precision floating-point value. In representing character arrays, many little men, each with a knapsack containing only one compartment to hold one byte of information, are domiciled at the same residence.

The following program will begin to explain our neighborhood designations:

```
/* SAMPLE */
main()
{

        int x;
        double y;
        long z;

        x = 34;
        y = 3712.8876;
        z = 123000;

        printf("%u  %u  %u\n", &x, &y, &z);

}
```

The neighborhood for this program consists of three little men and three houses. Mr. x, Mr. y, and Mr. z all live in the same neighborhood, each in a different house. Problem! We know that they live on "SAMPLE Street" in this neighborhood, but we don't know what their respective addresses are. The **printf()** function, as used in this program, can be likened to a neighborhood directory. The `&x`, `&y`, and `&z` designations are the addresses themselves. Therefore, at the beginning of each street in our fictitious neighborhood, there is the "PRINTF" directory with a movable arrow or "POINTER" with which to point to the names of Mr. x, Mr. y, and Mr. z. When the arrow is aimed at Mr. x, the directory displays his house address of 65504 SAMPLE Street. When the pointer is aimed at the name of Mr. y, the address of 65506 is displayed on the directory. Going through the same mechanics for Mr. z, we find that he lives at 65514 SAMPLE Street. (*Note:* These addresses are relatively arbitrary. The point to remember is that whenever the pointer that is a part of the street directory is aimed at a name, the address of that "person" is returned.)

Expanding on the previous program, we arrive at the following:

```
/* SAMPLE */
main()
{

        int x;
        double y;
        long z;
```

```
        x = 34;
        y = 3712.8876;
        z = 123000;

        printf("%u  %u  %u\n", &x, &y, &z);
        printf("%d %d %d\n", sizeof(x), sizeof(y), sizeof(z));
}
```

The added **printf()** line allows us to imagine another type of directory. The **sizeof()** function allows us to list the number of compartments each little man has in his knapsack. This separate directory lets us know that Mr. x has two compartments in his knapsack; Mr. y has eight compartments, and Mr. z has four compartments. These, of course, correspond to 2, 8, and 4 bytes of storage space for integer, double-precision floating-point, and long integer values.

Summary

This chapter has presented a very basic introduction to the essential processes that occur when a variable is declared and assigned. On declaration, an exclusive area of memory, retained specifically for storage of variables, is set aside. The number of bytes retained is dependent on the type of variable and can be as large as 8 bytes when dealing with standard types of variables and assuming the use of the Borland Turbo C compiler or nearly every C compiler used with an MS-DOS machine.

Each variable is associated with two distinct values. The most common is the object value, which is assigned to this variable by the program. The second value is the memory address of the variable. The latter can be obtained by using the unary ampersand (&) operator in connection with the variable name. Any assignments made to the variable are stored in the bytes that start at this memory address. While it is certainly easy and necessary to change the object value, since this is the true "variable" value, it is not possible to change the memory address of a declared variable. This is fixed and can be thought of as a constant after the variable has been initialized.

Auto variables in C, the type most used in this programming

language (as opposed to register and static variables), can be equal to any legal value when first declared and before any object values are assigned in the program. In other words, an auto variable has a random object value when first declared. This is true because, in C, declaring a variable simply causes the compiler to set aside storage space. The space reserved for this variable is not cleared to zero as is the case in some other languages.

The space set aside for the exclusive storage of each declared variable lies in a "safe" area of memory. This is a function of the compiler's memory management functions. This means that the area of memory used for this purpose is not shared by other services that could overwrite the variable's object values or be overwritten by object value assignments to the variable. Likewise, no two variables will be allocated storage at the same address (again, when dealing with the types of variables discussed in this point). These areas of memory, then, are exclusive and "safe," at least from intrusion by other "standard" variables.

Important! A standard variable can be assigned any legal object value. When dealing with numeric-type variables as have been discussed in this chapter, this means object assignments within the normal numeric range for the type of variable declared. Variable `x`, for instance, can be assigned a value of 14 and then reassigned a new value of 234. This can go on ad infinitum. However, the memory address of that variable is fixed. It cannot be reassigned. If storage for this variable is allocated at memory location 65514, then this is that variable's "fixed" address for the duration of the program. This cannot be changed.

I realize that most of this discussion may be old hat to more than a few readers. However, I have also worked with C programmers who have been at this game for quite a while and who still do not "visualize" the processes that take place during simple declaration and assignment operations. If you do not completely understand *all* of the discussions that have taken place in this chapter, then please reread these front pages. Their content is essential to the full understanding of the materials that are to follow. One shadow of doubt regarding this chapter can and will cause endless frustration and headaches in trying to fathom the remaining discussions.

Chapter 3

A Second Step to Learning Pointers

The previous chapter touched on the processes that take place, invisibly and internally, when declaring standard numeric variables in C language. This forms the start of a learning base from which to proceed into the full subject of C language pointers. This next chapter will expand on that base, broaden it, and make for a smoother transition into the depths of declaring pointers and using them to the best programming advantage.

C Language Character Arrays and C Strings

When dealing with character strings in C, we come closer and closer to pure pointer operations. However, C strings, or, more appropriately, arrays of characters, also bear a close similarity to working with numbers and with numeric-type variables. Therefore, the creation and use of character arrays in C is the next logical step in the discussion of pointers.

The following program will aid in this discussion:

```
main()
{
        char x;

        x = 65;

        printf("%c\n", x);

}
```

This program displays the letter "A" on the monitor screen, but as before, let's run through the invisible processes that take place when this simple program is executed.

The declaration line states that variable `x` is of type `char`. This means that a single byte is set aside for the exclusive use of this variable. The standard legal values for a char variable consist of unsigned integers in the range of 0 to 255. (*Note:* This has changed a bit in recent years. This subject will be discussed further in a later section.) Only 1 byte is required for any number in this range of values.

A value of 65, as is the case here, represents the uppercase "A" while "B" is 66, "C" is 67, and so on. The assignment line uses the ASCII numeric value, but this line could just as easily have been written as:

```
x = 'A';
```

In C terminology, the `'A'` designation means exactly the same thing as 65. Instead, `'A'` is automatically transposed by the compiler as 65.

The only reason why the `'A'` is displayed on the screen as a letter instead of a number is due to the `%c` designation in the

printf() format control line. This specifies that the value in its argument, x, be displayed as an ASCII character.

As was discussed in the previous chapter, the address of the 1 byte of storage allocated to char x can be returned by adding the program line:

```
printf("%u\n", &x);
```

Since only 1 byte of storage is allocated to a char-type variable in most C compilers intended for MS-DOS machines (and, for that matter, the great majority of all microcomputers), the address returned names this sole byte.

This sample program uses a char variable. However, such an application in a practical C program is rarely seen. Because of the conversions that take place in C, all chars are eventually converted to int types, just as all floats are converted to doubles. A single char variable is seldom used, even by functions that, for instance, capture a single character from the keyboard. One that comes to mind is **getchar().** This function temporarily halts execution until a single character is input via the keyboard and followed by a carriage return. The **getch()** function (in most implementations) does the same thing, but restarts the execution chain immediately after keyboard input scans the single character input. While both of these functions are available with the intent of returning single characters, a char variable should not be used as the return variable. The reason for this is that both of these functions will return a −1 value if an error occurs. By definition, a char variable is an unsigned type (although variations now occur in the newer ANSI standard compilers). An unsigned variable is not capable of "holding" a signed number as is the case with −1. For this reason alone, int-type variables are or should always be used.

The most commonly seen use of the char data type is in the char array, an array of characters that represents a string. A string is often treated as a single unit in many computer languages, and it can be handled in this same manner in C. However, C does not have a true string variable. All strings are stored as an array of individual units. These units are characters or chars, and each character in an array consumes 1 byte of storage in most implementations.

The following program demonstrates a most common use of the char array:

```
main()
{

        char x[9];

        strcpy(x, "COMPILER");

        printf("%s\n", x);

}
```

This program will display the string "COMPILER" on the monitor screen.

The invisible events are more numerous in this program. First of all, variable x is declared a char array composed of nine (9) consecutive storage bytes. Here, the programmer has direct control over how much storage space is set aside, whereas with all previous variables, the storage space was automatically set. As with the single char variable, storage is automatically set at 1 byte per character position, but here nine 1-byte array elements are specified in the declaration line. Therefore, nine SSUs (standard storage units) are allocated.

The reason for the selection of an array subscript of nine is due to the fact that the string constant, "COMPILER", is to be *copied* into the array. Now, this constant contains only eight (8) letters. The extra byte of storage is not just a safeguard. Rather, it is absolutely essential and not an extra byte at all.

The only element that makes COMPILER a true string in C and not just a consecutive trail of single characters is the operation of, in this program, the **strcpy()** function. This function is used to copy the characters that make up this constant to the memory positions set aside exclusively for array x[ ]. In C, the definition of a character string is "a single unit of characters terminated by a NULL character." The NULL character is ASCII zero (0). You don't see this character anywhere in the program, but the compiler automatically adds it to the end of the constant, `COMPILER`, during its operations. The **strcpy()** function also copies the NULL character into the ninth array byte. Therefore, the copy of the constant is written to the 9 consecutive bytes reserved for `x[]` as:

```
COMPILER\0
```

The `'\0'` is the NULL character and signals the end of the character string. The NULL character makes this combination of single characters into a single string, a unit that may be treated as a single entity instead of a grouping of characters.

Don't be confused into thinking that **strcpy()** purposely tacks on an extra `'\0'` to the end of the quoted string used as its argument when it copies this string into the reserved memory locations. While this could easily be arranged by rewriting or even writing a new version of **strcpy()**, it is not necessary.

One must remember that all constants written into a program that is to be compiled must be written somewhere in memory when the compiled program is actually executed. When the compiler sees the constant `"COMPILER"` in the source code, it causes it to be written somewhere with the executable code that is its output. When this program is executed, this string constant is written to a safe place somewhere in memory. It is stored as:

```
COMPILER\0
```

The compiler actually tacks on the NULL character, although it is never seen in the source code. Now, when the **strcpy()** function is invoked, it is handed the memory address of this constant and copies the contents from the constant's memory location into the bytes reserved for `x[]`. This includes the NULL character. As a matter of fact, encountering the NULL character is a signal to **strcpy()** to stop reading further bytes of information. When **strcpy()** has completed its run, there are two `COMPILER` strings in memory. One is the original constant, which we will say, for purposes of discussion, is contained in the bytes that begin at memory address 61000 *and* the copy produced by **strcpy()** at, again for discussion purposes only, memory address 64115.

Proceeding further, when **printf()** is handed a control string argument of `%s`, this is a signal telling it that it is to expect a pointer argument. In this example, `x`, used without the braces, is that pointer argument. **Printf()** goes to that memory address and starts reading a string. But it does this a single character at a time. It writes each byte to the screen as an ASCII character. It will do this forever *or* until it intercepts the NULL byte (`\0`). When this occurs, **printf()** stops reading this location and either exits or goes to another argument if the format string indicates that another is available. In this example, there are no other arguments, so **printf()** is exited.

The first question that comes to mind is "Where did **printf()** get a pointer argument?" This is a valid question, since there are no ampersands and no specifically declared pointers in this program. The answer lies in how C handles char arrays. The construct `x[0]`, for instance, is a bona fide variable. It represents or returns the character in the first position of array `x`. However, when `x` is used without a subscript, it then becomes a *pointer* to the address of the first character in the string. Remember:

A char array name, when used without the subscript brackets, is a pointer to the start of the array storage and returns the memory location of the first byte, which is also the start of the string. It does not return the contents of that byte. It returns the byte's address in memory!

It can be safely said that `x[0]` is a variable. It can be reassigned any legal object value as in:

```
x[0] = 66;
```

This reassigns the first character in our string the letter "B." If this line were inserted into our program between **strcpy()** and **printf()**, then `"BOMPILER"` would be displayed on the screen. However, `x`, used without subscript brackets, is a pointer. It does not return the contents of a byte; rather, it returns the memory address of the start of the string.

The ampersand unary operator cannot be used in a construct of:

```
&x
```

because `x` is already a pointer. However, it can be used with a variable as in:

```
&x[0]
```

Remember, `x[0]` is a variable and `&x[0]` returns the memory address of this variable, the first byte in the array. This also happens to be the same address returned by `x`, the pointer to the start of the array. By the same token, `&x[1]` returns the address of the second byte in the array. It is a pointer to the address of this second byte.

Here is another way the former program example could be written:

```
main()
{

        char x[9];
        int i;

        x[0] = 'C';
        x[1] = 'O';
        x[2] = 'M';
        x[3] = 'P';
        x[4] = 'I';
        x[5] = 'L';
        x[6] = 'E';
        x[7] = 'R';
        x[8] = '\0';

        i = 0;
        while (x[i] != '\0')
                putchar(x[i++];

}
```

This program does exactly what the previous one did, but replaces **strcpy()** with direct assignment lines. The **while** loop provides a very rough idea of how **printf()** works when displaying a string on the screen. Within the loop clause, termination instructions are given. The **while** loop will cycle as long as `x[i]` is not equal to zero. Note that `x[8]` is assigned a NULL value that equates to decimal zero. **Putchar** is used to display a single character on the screen during each pass. On each of these passes, variable `i` is incremented by one. When `i` is finally incremented to a value of 8, `x[i]` or `x[8]` is equal to zero (NULL) and the **while** loop is exited.

However, the analogy this latter program bears to the first one breaks down on close examination. In the latter example, no pointer operations were used. In the former, pointers are everywhere. *Don't . . . don't . . . don't* ever think that, in the original program, `x` returns the string. This is totally untrue. It should be understood that C language doesn't really have any true string variables. There are *none.* However, C devises a way in which functions may access a series of characters until a stopping point is reached. This stopping point is signaled by the NULL character. Again `x` does not equal `"COMPILER"`. It only returns the memory address at which the first character in this array is stored. Functions that accept this pointer are programmed to be "smart" and know to quit what they are doing after reading the NULL character. This next program will help demonstrate this point:

```
main()
{

        char x[9];

        strcpy(x, "COMPILER");

        printf("%u\n", x);
        printf("%s\n", x);
        printf("%s\n", &x[0]);

}
```

When executed, this program will display:

```
65508
COMPILER
COMPILER
```

The first value is the memory address of the start of the array. If you try this program on your machine, the actual address may vary in value from what is shown here. Regardless, the address is that of the start of the array. The next line displays `COMPILER`. This occurs because the `%s` conversion specification handed to **printf()** causes the function to look for a memory address and then to display the contents at this address, consecutively and continuously until the NULL character is read. Now, `COMPILER` is displayed again. *Why?*

Earlier, it was stated that `x` is a pointer that returns the address of the first element in the array. It was also stated that `x[0]` is a variable and `&x[0]` is a pointer to that variable's memory location. Since this is the first variable in the array, its address is the same as the starting address of the array. In the last **printf()** line, a `%s` conversion specification was the only argument in the format string. Therefore, a pointer or memory address is expected. This criterion is met by `&x[0]`, and the full contents of the array are displayed. It can be readily observed that `x`, the pointer; and `&x[0]`, the pointer, both point to the same place in memory. They are one and the same.

This occurrence is not unusual. C language had this feature written in by its designers. Using the array name without the subscript is just a shorthand method of stating the same thing that is stated with `&x[0]`. This is easier on the programmer, since less typing is required, but it sometimes tends to confuse beginners. If you want to have some fun, try to guess what the following program displays:

```
main()
{

        char x[9];
```

```
            strcpy(x, "COMPILER");

            printf("%s\n", &x[3]);

        }
```

The answer is "PILER". Since the argument to **printf()** is the memory address of the fourth character in the array (remember, we start counting array elements at 0 not 1), the byte read by **printf()** begins at the letter "P." As was stated before, **printf()** is only given a starting point in memory to begin reading byte contents. It reads these contents until a NULL character is reached. Since the read began at "P" and the NULL occurs after the "R," only this portion of the original string constant that was copied into the memory location reserved for array x is displayed.

It is important to state again that, in this context, x is a pointer and does not equal any object value (at least in the way we think of objects as opposed to addresses). It returns only the address of a memory location where objects have been written. It certainly does not equal "COMPILER" or even the first letter of this string. It is the equivalent of &x[0], which is also a pointer. Both x and &x[0] point to the same memory location.

It should also be made clear that the array is in no way equal to the *constant,* "COMPILER". Rather, this array contains an exact copy of the bytes that make up this constant. The constant that was an argument to **strcpy()** lies at one place in memory, and the copy that was brought about by **strcpy()** lies at another. This is extremely important in understanding pointer operations, which will be discussed a bit later. **Strcpy()** is an aptly named function. It copies consecutive bytes of data. A "copy" indicates that there must be an original. The constant is this original and the contents of the array are the copy. Both exist simultaneously in computer memory and at different memory addresses. This is not a figurative statement but a true-life fact.

Lack of Array Bounds Checking

One of the touted weaknesses of the C programming language is the lack of array bounds checking. This is the cost of relatively frugal use of memory, a strong point of C. Lack of bounds checking simply means that there are no safeguards that prevent an array from being overwritten. If a char array is declared with a subscript of, say, nine positions, then only 9 sequential bytes of memory are *reserved* for storage to this array. However, if a programmer miscalculates and writes more than nine characters (including the NULL) to this array, the excess characters are written into the memory locations that immediately follow those that were reserved. The nine-element boundary of the array is passed, and bytes are written into memory locations not set aside exclusively for this array. When this occurs, what happens?

There is no single answer to this question. If there are few declared variables in the program, then there is a good chance that the unreserved portion of memory that was overwritten by the offending string is not being used anyway. The program may run in a normal fashion. However, if there are many variables, there is a very good chance that the exclusive storage allocated to these other variables may be overwritten by the long string. This will certainly cause an improper execution sequence. A worst-case scenario might involve those extra string elements overwriting a "management" portion of memory or even interacting with other variables to do the same thing. The result here can be a "crash," where the computer simply locks up and must be rebooted. However, there have been cases where hard-disk drives have been erased by inadvertent overwrites to interrupt addresses, a disaster.

Overwriting an array is the exact equivalent of writing a program that simply pokes random values into random memory locations. This is a crap shoot and anything goes! Obviously, this situation can bring about possible disasters such as the hard-disk example. Don't overwrite array boundaries!!!

The following program illustrates what can happen in an array overwrite:

```
main()
{

      char a[3], b[10];

      strcpy(a, "LANGUAGE"); /* Overwrite */
      strcpy(b, "COMPILER");
```

```
    printf("%s\n", a);
    printf("%s\n", b);

}
```

The expectation here is the display of:

```
LANGUAGE
COMPUTER
```

However, the **strcpy()** assignment to array a is an overwrite! Three array elements were reserved for storage by the assignment:

```
char a[3]
```

But LANGUAGE consists of eight characters and will consume 8 bytes of storage. We must also take into account the NULL character (\0) for a total of 9 bytes. The array bounds are exceeded, and there will be no error message or warning when the program compiles. Using the Turbo C compiler in small-memory-model mode on the reference microcomputer system, this program will display:

```
LANGCOMPILER
COMPILER
```

The reason for this lies in the way storage is managed. Array a was allocated 3 bytes of storage at memory location 65504 in the 64K segment. Array b was allocated 10 storage bytes at 65508. Here is what happened. LANGUAGE was written in memory starting at 65504. Owing to the fact that 9 storage bytes were required to contain this string, bytes 65504 through 65510 were utilized. But allocated storage for array b began at 65508, so the supposedly exclusive storage allocation for this latter array was intruded on. However, LANGUAGE was still written to memory. This would have been fine if the assignment to array b had not been made . . . but it was made. When the second **strcpy()** function was executed, it began writing COMPILER at address 65508. Therefore, this last string was written over the portion of the first string that intruded into its exclusive storage area.

Such an overwrite was not in any way disastrous in this simple program. Additionally, the error was immediately recognizable and can be easily corrected by allocating more storage space to array `a`; however, if this program had been more complex, an overwrite of this nature could have led to hours upon hours of debugging.

This simple example should provide a very worthwhile lesson in array handling. This lesson will carry over (but magnified 100-fold) when dealing with declared pointers.

The "Little Man" Method

In the fictitious neighborhood discussed in the last chapter, there is a small town composed of many little houses in which reside little men with knapsacks on their backs. Some knapsacks have several compartments for storing bytes; some have fewer. The little man that represents a char variable has a very small knapsack. It contains only a single compartment for the storage of 1 byte. The following program will aid in this story:

```
/* CHARACTERS */

main()
{

        char c;
        c = 'A';
        printf("%u\n", &c);
        printf("%c\n", c);

}
```

As before, we know the name of the little man (`c`), but we don't know where he lives, so we use the **PRINTF()** electronic directory at the corner of CHARACTERS Street. The ampersand pointer, when aimed at `c`'s name, returns the address where `c` lives.

On this same street, there is a townhouse complex, in which the units are all tied together but also separate from each other. This domicile will provide a storybook example of the char array demonstrated by the following program:

```
main()
{

        char c[9];

        strcpy(c, "COMPILER");

        printf("%u\n", c);
        printf("%s\n", c);

}
```

In this townhouse development, there are nine units. In each of the first eight units, one little man resides. All of these little men are brothers, and all have the same last name, which happens to be `c`. Since we know the last name, the POINTER on the street-corner directory is aimed at `c`. (Remember, `c` without the brackets is a pointer. The ampersand is unnecessary.) This gives us the address of the first townhouse in the complex, 65504 CHARACTERS Street. The first-born brother lives in the first townhouse (`&c[0]`), the second-born in townhouse number 2 (`&c[1]`), and so on. Remember, there are only eight brothers but nine townhouses in this complex. The last townhouse (`&c[8]`) is vacant. The last **printf()** line in the above program represents a special feature that is a part of this townhouse directory. It will allow us to see the contents of each brother's knapsack. When this directory is implemented, the content of each knapsack is displayed in sequential order. The contents are sampled as long as there are knapsacks available. However, when the ninth townhouse is reached in this "poll," it is empty. There is no little man and, of course, no knapsack. The special directory scan is halted.

Incidentally, if we want to know the address of an individual brother, we would utilize the standard ampersand pointer that is also available at this street-corner directory and point to the desired brother's name. Their names are `c[0]`, `c[1]`, `c[2]`, `c[3]`, `c[4]`, `c[5]`, `c[6]`, and `c[7]`. Therefore, placing the ampersand in front of the proper brother's name will yield his address. Placing the "display" feature of this directory on an individual brother's name (no ampersand here) reveals the contents of this individual's knapsack.

At this point in the discussion, we will forego further formal use of the "little man" method, although he will appear now and then at a particularly crucial point in future discussions. It is hoped that this "storybook" approach has enabled any reader who may have had conceptual difficulties with the front matter of the preceding chapters to get the correct "feel" of the operations under study. However, it is very essential that the basics outlined in this text so far be fully understood. If necessary, reread any materials that may not be second-nature to you in order to clear up these gray areas of misunderstanding.

Summary

It can be seen that, unlike single-element variables, char arrays offer more sampling variations. We can find the address of the start of the array by using the array name, `c`, which is a pointer to the start of array storage as an argument to a **printf()** function that contains the `&u` conversion specifier. We can also display the entire contents of this array by using `c` again, still a pointer, as an argument to a **printf()** function that contains a `%s` conversion specifier. To continue, the address of any single element in the array can be obtained by using the ampersand unary operator in front of the array name followed by its bracketed subscript. Here, it will be necessary to use the `%u` specifier again. If we merely want the object stored by a single array element, the element name without the ampersand is used with a `%c` specifier (for the display of a single ASCII character).

For all intents and purposes, each element in a char array may be treated exactly like a standard variable of type int, except that only 1 byte of storage is allocated instead of 2. However, the entire contents or combined contents of the array may also be accessed as a single unit. This provides great flexibility, uncommon to many other languages, and should not add a great deal of confusion if you are aware of the two-part nature of character arrays. The first part is that of a group of individual values. The second is the string, which is all of these values rolled into a single unit.

Chapter 4

Declared Pointers and Their Operations

Pointers are special variables that return the address of a memory location. This statement has been repeated again and again. There is nothing especially mysterious about pointers and what they do, but initial concepts often breed their own mysteries. This may be the real problem with programmers and pointers.

The discussions in the opening chapters of this text have expanded on some very basic operations in the C programming language. Hopefully, the reader has gained an added or, at least, a reinforced insight into the memory management that takes place in even the simplest programs. These insights will be a great aid in feeling comfortable with the discussions that are to follow.

All of the pointers that have been discussed to this juncture have been "fixed"; that is, they have been inextricably tied to a variable that was declared at the opening of the program. This chapter deals with variables that are declared from the onset to be pointers. These variables do not store objects, at least as we think of them in regard to other variables. They store an address of a memory location.

Unlike the pointers discussed previously, these can be made to point to any area of memory.

The following program will begin the exploration into this area of declared pointers in C language programs:

```
main()
{

        int i, *p;

        i = 43;
        p = &i;

        printf("%d %d\n", i, *p);

}
```

The declaration line of this program names i a variable of type int. The same line also declares that p is a pointer. The unary asterisk (*) operator is the key here. The declaration indicates that the combination of this operator and variable p is an int data type. This, then, is a pointer that is structured to point to an address in memory that contains or can contain a legal int value.

I realize that the opening of this discussion may be very confusing, but bear with me and clarity should prevail. Just remember for now that i is an int variable and p is a declared pointer of type int.

In the next program segment, int variable i is assigned a value of 43 decimal. The following line assigns the pointer (p) the address of the storage allocated to the previous variable. After these assignments have been made, variable i contains an object of 43 . . . and p points to the first byte of memory allocated to i.

When the **printf()** function is called, it is handed two arguments. Both of these are decimal integers as is indicated by the %d conversion specifiers used in **printf**'s format control clause. The screen will display:

```
43 43
```

These two values are one and the same. **Printf()** got these two arguments from the same memory location. When the declarations were made, variable i was allocated 2 bytes of storage for a standard integer. Pointer p was allocated only enough memory to contain a memory address. This is all a pointer can do. In a standard variable, we have learned to expect an object and a memory address. In a pointer, the object is a memory address, and like any other object, this memory address can be changed. Here is a special variable that seems to have the capability of moving through memory. This is true, based on appearances, and for the time being we will follow this concept.

As important as the ability to move around in memory can be, using the unary * operator, we can retrieve bytes of data from wherever the pointer is pointing or even write new data to that area of memory.

The simple program under discussion usually leads to more questions than it answers, but it's a place to start. One question always asked is how this program differs from the following one:

```
main()
{

        int i, p;

        i = p = 43;

        printf("%d   %d\n", i, p);

}
```

This causes the two copies of the constant (43) to be stored in memory. One of these 43s is stored at the memory address set aside for exclusive storage to variable i. Another copy is made at the memory address set aside for variable p.

We have just seen how a declared pointer may be used to return the object value from the memory location to which it is directed to point. The following example shows how the pointer may be utilized to write a value to the same memory location:

```
main()
{

        int i, *p;

        i = 43;
        p = &i;

        *p = 16;

        printf("%d\n", i);

}
```

When this program is compiled and executed, it will display:

```
16
```

on the monitor screen. Note that variable i is assigned a value of 43 in this program, but when it is passed as an argument to **printf()**, this value has been changed. Variable i is now equal to 16. The reason for this lies in the pointer operation. After the declaration line, assignments are made. Variable i is assigned a value of 43, and the pointer, p, is assigned the memory address of this variable. This means that p points to the exclusive storage set aside for variable i. However, another assignment line uses the unary * operator in connection with the pointer. This combination is the object value at the memory location. *p accesses the byte contents at the memory address and is an integer. Now, these contents are reassigned to a value of 16. This means that the value of 43 is overwritten and in its place is the value of 16. Since this is the area of storage for i, the object value of i is changed. This is true, although no reassignments were made directly by using the i variable.

Throughout the discussion of declared pointers, the pointer has always been assigned the address of a declared int variable by using the unary & operator in conjunction with the variable name. We have already learned that this returns the memory address of the storage set aside for the variable. However, if the specific memory location of this variable is already known, the address assignment to the pointer can be made directly and numerically. The following program illustrates this. To be fully understood, you must assume that it has been determined that the storage address of `int` variable `i` is 65514. Just how this is determined is not important, relevant, or possibly even accurate. But, for the sake of discussion, we will assume this to be the correct address of variable `i` on declaration:

```
main()
{

        int i, *p;

        p = (int *) 65514;
        *p = 78;

        printf("%d\n", i);

}
```

When this program is executed, the object value of `i` will, indeed, be 67, the value assigned to the memory location to which `p` points. You will observe that when the pointer is assigned a memory address value, a cast operator is used in the form of `(int *)`. This operator casts or coerces the numeric value (an unsigned integer constant) into an int pointer type. Most compilers will issue warnings if this cast operator is not used, and some will consider it an error not to include it. The Borland Turbo C compiler, which is used as the model compiler for this text, considers it an error, so the cast operator is mandatory.

Be aware that the assignment line:

```
p = (int *) 65514;
```

is exactly equivalent to:

```
p = &i;
```

if we assume that the memory address of variable `i` is at 65514 in the 64K data segment.

A Practical Use of Pointers

The program examples to this point have been of very little practical value other than as simple tutorials to teach the basics of pointer operations. This discussion will delve into some practical uses of pointers, utilizing them in constructs where no other type of variable will serve nearly so well.

Every beginning C programmer at one time or another has tried to do what is illustrated in the following program:

```
main()
{

        int x;

        x = 23;

        change(x);

        printf("%d\n", x);

}
change(x)
int x;
{

        x = 148;

}
```

This program is very simplistic and absolutely incorrect. The attempt here is to change the object value of a variable from within a customized (programmer-written) function. This simply can't be done. When this program is executed, it will display the value of 23 on the screen. The operations that take place within the function have no bearing whatsoever on the object value of the variable that was passed to **change()**.

In the C programming language, arguments are passed to functions "by value." This simply means that the value of the variable x in the above example (23) is passed to the **change()** function. The function variable, also named x, is a discrete entity, having no relationship whatsoever with the other x variable in the main portion of this program.

All a C function can do is to return a value to the calling program. It cannot change the object value by acting on the value of a standard variable. However, pointers allow us to make the in-memory changes attempted by the previous program. Using pointers, the program could be written correctly as:

```
main()
{

        int x;

        x = 23;

        change(&x);

        printf("%d\n", x);

}
change(x)
int *x;
{

        *x = 148;

}
```

This will work as originally intended. The value displayed on the screen will be 148. The program is set up as before, but the **change()** function is passed the "memory address" of variable x, instead of its object value. Within the body of the **change()** function, the passed value is declared a pointer of type `int` by the line:

```
int *x;
```

Now, the object value at this memory location, `*x`, is reassigned a value of 148. The function has been able to locate the exclusive storage area for variable x in the calling program, change it, and then relinquish control to the calling program. Incidentally, the **change()** function used the name x as its pointer variable just as the former, incorrect, example did. This is certainly not mandatory or even desirable. The **change()** function could just as easily have been written as:

```
change(i)
int *i;
{

        *i = 148;

}
```

A function is a completely separate program from that managed under the auspices of **main().** The variables, pointers or otherwise, within a function are not the same variables that are contained in the calling program, even though they may have the same names. In this last program, the **change()** function actually creates another pointer of type int that is assigned the same memory address as the pointer that was passed from the calling program. There are two pointers at work here, and each points to the same memory location. While there are two pointers, one under **main()** and one under **change(),** they both point to the same memory location. A change in object value stored at this single location has the same effect, regardless of which pointer was used to effect the operation. The pointer within the function was used to change the value at the memory address allocated to x in the main program. The variable in the calling program is used by **printf()** to display the object value.

Note that the memory address of the variable in the calling program is passed as &x, using the unary & operator to obtain the pointer argument. In the function, the pointer is "declared" in the standard fashion using the unary * operator. The argument is passed to the function as a "fixed" pointer (fixed to the variable), whereas the pointer variable within the function is declared a pointer from the start.

Perhaps the best illustration of the use of a pointer to make object changes to the calling program from within a function is the **swap()** function, first discussed in "The C Programming Language." An example of this is illustrated in the following program:

```
main()
{

        int x, y;

        x = 10;
        y = 127;

        swap(&x, &y);

        printf("%d   %d\n", x, y);

}
swap(a, b)
int *a, *b;
{

        int i;

        i = *a;
        *a = *b;
        *b = i;

}
```

Again, addresses are passed from the calling program to the **swap()** function. These arguments are declared int pointers within the function, which also declares an internal variable of type int. The latter is a standard auto variable and not a pointer. Variable i is used to temporarily hold the object value of *a. Remember, when used in this context, *a is the object value of the bytes stored at the memory location pointed to by a. The unary * operator dictates this type of return. Next, the object at the memory address pointed to by pointer a is reassigned the object value that resides in the memory location held by pointer b. Again, the unary * operators are used to access the objects at the memory addresses as opposed to the address, proper. Finally, the bytes pointed to by b are reassigned the value in i. The swap is complete and the program will display:

```
127   10
```

since the object values of x and y in the calling program have been swapped.

Danger!!!

Some of the dangers of pointer operations were alluded to in earlier chapters. Since pointers can be directed to other areas of memory, one must make certain that those areas are safe—that is, not used for other purposes of which the programmer may have no knowledge. In the last few program examples, declared pointers were always given the address of existing variables as in:

```
p = &i
```

Here p is a declared pointer and i is an int variable that was also declared. Since storage was specifically allocated to i on its declaration, it's okay for the pointer to point to this memory address. Then, the pointer can only retrieve or be used to rewrite the contents of i. The following program demonstrates a very dangerous use of a pointer, and is indicative of some things programmers inexperienced with pointers sometimes do:

```
main()
{

        int *x;

        *x = 10;

        printf("%d\n", *x);

}
```

Here, a pointer of type `int` is declared followed by an assignment to a value of 10. Remember, a pointer always points to a memory location. When a pointer is used to assign an object to memory, as is the case here, we must know where in memory that assignment is made. The big question here is to what or where `x` points? The answer is . . . it's anybody's guess!!!

It was previously learned that when a standard auto variable (of type int for this discussion) is declared, memory is set aside for its exclusive storage. It was also learned that the bytes at this storage location are not cleared to zero and may contain any value on a more or less random basis. The same is true of pointers.

However, the object value of a pointer is a memory address. Therefore, when a pointer is declared, the address it contains . . . the area of memory to which it points . . . can be any random value of from 0 to 65536 (assuming use of a small-memory-model compiler using 2-byte pointers). Here again is the proverbial crap shoot. If you have ever written and run a program along the lines of this latter example, you were writing things to memory locations not reserved for that purpose. You were *POKE*ing around in memory at random.

There's a pretty good chance that, if your program was simple and small, like this example, nothing unusual took place, and the program ran as expected. All this means is that you got lucky!

There is also the possibility that your machine locked up and had to be rebooted or even that another part of your program was trashed.

When objects are written to random memory locations, anything and everything can and does happen. This sort of programming error is exactly equivalent to the array overwrite discussed in the last chapter, and must be avoided at all costs.

Other Pointers of Numeric Types

The examples of declared pointer operations discussed to this point in this chapter have all been of type int. This simply means that the declared pointer expects to point to a memory location that contains or will contain a value within the range of a standard integer. The previous **swap()** function allowed the values of two int variables in the calling program to be exchanged. However, this same function would not work if handed the addresses of, say, double variables.

In the C programming language, a pointer can be of many different data types. The following program shows how the previous **swap()** function needs to be altered in order to exchange the values of two double variables:

```
main()
{
        double x, y;

        x = 14.673;
        y = 0.39712349;

        swap(&x, &y);

        printf("%lf   %lf\n", x, y);

}
```

```
swap(a, b)
double *a, *b;
{

        double i;

        i = *a;
        *a = *b;
        *b = i;

}
```

The only change in the function, proper, is that the pointer variables have been declared `double` instead of `int`. The internally declared variable `i` is also changed to a double-precision floating-point type. Everything else remains the same. Of course, the arguments passed to **swap()** are the addresses of double variables declared in the calling program.

While it is proper for the programmer to be thinking in terms of memory addresses when dealing with pointers, it is equally important to know what kind of object is to be written or returned via the use of pointers. One would no more expect to read from or assign a double value to a memory location set aside for an int value than to assign the object value of a double directly to an int-type variable.

Summary

This chapter has dealt with only the basics of declaring pointers of numeric data types. In each case, the declared pointers were used to point to the location of the same type of auto variable. This is known as "initializing" a pointer, causing it to point to a known memory location.

When a pointer is declared, it is uninitialized, just as is the case with a declared auto variable. Therefore, an uninitialized pointer has a random object value, the object being a memory address. An uninitialized pointer, then, can point to any area of memory. This makes it a potentially "dangerous" item that can wreak havoc with a program. An uninitialized pointer is exactly like an auto variable that has been declared but has not been assigned any value.

Remember, a pointer is declared for the specific purpose of storing the address of a known memory location. A known memory location may be specified by the programmer in two different ways. The direct method entails constructs similar to:

```
x = (int *) 65117;
```

In this example, 65117 was chosen arbitrarily. It is assumed that the programmer has a specific need or desire to access this location. The indirect method might be written as follows:

```
x = &y;
```

where `x` is a pointer and `y` is a declared variable with automatic storage set aside for its objects.

Both of these methods return a numeric address to the pointer. The first is specified as a constant, while the second method retrieves an address by using the unary `&` operator with a variable. We don't necessarily know the specific address using the latter method, but the pointer does, and that's what's important.

Pointers are very useful as arguments to functions that must access memory locations within the calling program. Remember, arguments are passed to functions by value. Without pointers, functions could do no more than pass values back to the calling program. With pointers, functions can change values in memory that affect the calling program with no further actions on the part of the latter.

The use of the unary `*` operator with a pointer name causes the object value at the memory address stored in the pointer to be returned. Also, the object value may be changed by making a new assignment via the pointer and the unary operator. When used with this operator, the pointer may be treated exactly like an auto variable of the type under which the pointer was initially declared.

It must again be stressed that a pointer really holds nothing with the exception of a memory address. This is its object value. It does not hold a string, it does not hold an integer, it does not hold a double. In this regard, it doesn't hold anything. It "points" to a place in memory, and through the use of proper operators, the object values at the place to which it points can be retrieved or rewritten.

A pointer is not fixed to any single memory location. It can be directed to "rove" throughout the entire quantity of RAM (random-access memory). *Note:* The examples of pointers discussed to this point assume the use of a small-memory-model compiler option. Using MS-DOS, the small-memory models are confined to a 64K segment of memory for data storage. As such, they cannot be made to point to locations outside of this segment. The reason for this is that small-memory compiler model pointers are assigned 2 bytes to store a memory address. Within 2 bytes, the maximum unsigned value is 65536. Today, even budget MS-DOS machines are usually equipped with at least 256K memory and most are fully loaded at 640K. The latter configuration offers memory addresses 10 times larger than the 64K limitation placed on small-memory-model compilers.

Later discussions in this text will bring into play large-memory-model compilers, but the reader should understand that the small-memory models are most desirable, since they are the most efficient. This means that they produce compiled programs with the smallest object code size and generally run faster than those compiled with large-memory models. Sometimes it's necessary to forego these qualities for the "all-memory" access feature of the large-memory models. As a rule, however, use the small-memory model compilers wherever possible. Again, a lot more discussion will be devoted to this subject a bit later on.

Chapter 5

String Pointers

The previous chapter dealt with declared pointers of numeric types. That is, the pointer can be used to return an object value of one of the standard numeric data types, assuming that it is made to point to an area of memory containing this type of data. This chapter deals with the char or string pointer, one of the most common types of pointers seen in C language programs.

In C language, a pointer may be declared as any legal data type, including char. The char pointer is an often-used instrument for accessing and returning character strings. An earlier discussion of char arrays and their capabilities will come to light again in many of these discussions. For most purposes, char arrays and char pointers may be treated identically, especially in regard to being passed as arguments to functions. During the earlier discussion, it was learned that the name of a char array (without the use of the subscripting brackets) is indeed a pointer to the start of that array. In C, arrays of characters may be treated as strings by terminating the series of characters with a NULL (\0). The NULL is what identifies a character string as opposed to a sequential order of individual characters. The NULL is used for purposes of reading the string as a single unit.

The following program demonstrates the declaration of a char pointer and a potential use:

```
main()
{
        char a[40], *p;

        strcpy(a, "DATA");

        p = a;

        printf("%s\n", p);

}
```

This program will display the string, DATA, on the monitor screen, because p points to the start of the 40 sequential bytes of memory allocated to array a. As with previous pointer declarations, the unary * operator is used when declaring a char pointer. The **strcpy()** function copies a string constant into the bytes allocated to the array. Next, p is assigned the address of the array. When **printf()** gets the argument, it is a pointer to a string in memory.

Note that the ampersand operator was not used with the array in making the address assignment to pointer, p. Remember, a is the name of the array and is also a pointer, itself, when used without the brackets. Therefore, a returns an address to p, which is expecting one. While totally unnecessary, the pointer assignment line could have been written as:

```
p = &a[0];
```

This would assign p the same address as before, since this is the address returned by the original assignment line. You won't see an assignment like the latter in most C programs, as it is redundant.

The previous program displays the string pointed to by p on the screen when used as an argument to **printf()**. We know that p, the pointer, has exactly the same significance as a, the array name, which is also a pointer because of the lack of brackets. We also know that:

```
printf("%c\n", a[0]);
```

will return the first character in the string to **printf()**, where it will be displayed as a single character. To do the same thing with the pointer, the following program would suffice:

```
main()
{

        char a[40], *p;

        strcpy(a, "DATA");

        p = a;

        printf("%c\n", *c);

}
```

We need an object value as an argument to **printf()** when the `%c` conversion specifier is part of the format string. The designation `a[0]` is such an object value, and so is `*p`, which returns the object value at the single memory location pointed to by `p`.

In each of these examples, the declared pointer is always initialized by making it point to the memory location of a declared array. We can say that the pointer points to a "safe" area of memory that is composed of 40 consecutive bytes, since this is the subscript value of the array. However, both of the above programs can be made much simpler and will consume less memory by resorting to the following programming mode:

```
main()
{

        char *p;
```

```
        p = "DATA";

        printf("%s\n", p);

}
```

This program does exactly the same thing as the first example in this chapter, but it does not require the declaration of a char array. it does not use the **strcpy()** function, and it's simpler to write. From a memory standpoint, we are dealing with only a single variable, and that one is a pointer.

"But you assigned a pointer an object value and the pointer wasn't initialized!"

Hopefully, that may have been the first reaction the reader had to this program. And it would seem that we have done just that. After all, p wasn't made to point to a char array declared in the program. Or was it?

This program is perfectly correct, but it can lead to confusion, since it seems to go against everything that has been previously stated about the use of pointers.

First let's answer the question regarding initializing a pointer by giving it the address of a specific area of memory instead of the random value to which it points when first declared. It has been previously stated that C does not make any great provisions for strings. The only difference between a series of separate characters and a string is that the string is terminated by the NULL character. This is exactly what occurs when a string CONSTANT is included in a C program. This program uses the constant "DATA", which is surrounded by quotation marks, usually referred to as "double quotes" in C jargon. This constant must be stored at a memory location when the program is executed, and it is to this location that p is made to point by the assignment line:

```
p = "DATA";
```

This doesn't assign to p the object value of "DATA", only the address of the memory location where the constant has been stored. Therefore, p does point to a safe area of memory, the area where the constant was stored. Most programmers can grasp the concept of memory being set aside exclusively for declared variables, but memory is also set aside to store constants. Since a pointer may be directed to point to different areas of memory, it is just as easy to make it point to an area used to store a constant as it is to point to an area of memory allocated for use by a variable.

This sample program is only slightly different from the one that follows:

```
main()
{

        printf("%s\n", "DATA");

}
```

We already know that the %s conversion specification tells **printf()** to expect a char pointer argument, a pointer to the start of a string in memory. The objects at this memory location will be read and displayed on the screen as single characters until the NULL is encountered. Therefore, "DATA" is a pointer. In the former program, p will contain the same address as "DATA". If you don't fully understand this, the following program may help:

```
main()
{

        printf("%u\n", "DATA");

}
```

This program will display the memory address where the first letter in the string constant is stored. On my system, the address is at memory location 162 in the 64K data segment. This storage location will change slightly by also declaring a char pointer, as is the case with the following program:

```
main()
{

        char *p;

        p = "DATA";

        printf("%u\n", p);

}
```

On my system, address 158 is displayed which means that "DATA" was stored at locations 158, 159, 160, and 161 and the NULL character, at 162. One might think that this could be confirmed by printing the address of p and the address of "DATA" in the same **printf()** line. The following program is an example of how one might try to accomplish this goal, but it won't work:

```
main()
{

        char *p;

        p = "DATA";

        printf("%u  %u\n", p, "DATA");

}
```

This won't work the way many programmers expect it to. The idea here is that two identical memory addresses will be displayed on the screen. No way! The two addresses will be different. Why? The reason for this lies in the absolute fact that two different constants are used in this program. The first use of "DATA" is not equal to the second use of "DATA". Although both constants are identical in their character makeup, they are two discrete constants, each stored at a different location. Pointer p has been assigned the memory address of the first constant. The second constant is stored at a different address. Therefore, the address of p is different from the address of the constant used as an argument to **printf().** The address of p is the same as that of the first constant.

The char pointer in C is a very valuable commodity that will aid the programmer in many endeavors that include more than displaying or accessing string data. Such pointers are often required as arguments to functions that perform mass "peek/poke" operations and other forms of memory management in general.

Unlike the int pointer, which can be used to read or write a 2-byte quantity, char pointers address areas of memory a single byte at a time. That is, a char variable is allocated 1 byte, and a char array with a subscript of 40 allocates 40 single and consecutive bytes of data for its exclusive storage. Therefore, a standard C function such as **malloc()** will often return an address to a char pointer in order for that pointer to be used for single-byte access. The subject of memory allocation functions and pointers will be fully discussed in a later chapter.

Returning to earlier statements regarding the treatment of char pointers in the same manner as char arrays, observe the following program example:

```
main()
{

        char a[5];
        int x;

        strcpy(a, "DATA");

        for (x = 0; x <= 4; ++x)
             printf("%c\n", a[x]);

}
```

This program will display:

```
D
A
T
A
```

It does this by accessing each character in the array and treating it as a single entity. The bracketed subscript is advanced by the stepping of the loop so that characters in array positions 0 to 4 are read independently by each loop cycle. Here, the string value is unimportant (as a string, proper). The idea is to access each character on an individual basis.

This same operation can be done more efficiently by using a char pointer. The pointer equivalent of the previous program follows:

```
main()
{

        char *a;
        int x;

        a = "DATA";

        for (x = 0; x <= 4; ++x)
                printf("%c\n", *(a + x));

}
```

The key to this operation lies in the use of the unary `*` operator in conjunction with the pointer value added to the loop variable value. If `a` is a pointer with the address of a string, then `a + 1` is the address of that same string plus 1. For instance, if the address in `a` is 128, then `a + 1` is equal to 129 or memory address 129. Taking this further, if `a` is the address of the start of a string, then `a + 1` is the address one character into the string.

Likewise, if `*a` returns the first character in a string, then `*(a + 1)` returns the second character in the string. The parentheses are necessary in order to establish order of precedence from a purely mathematical standpoint.

It can be seen that `*(a + 3)` is the same as `b[3]`, assuming that `b` is a char array whose address is contained in pointer `a`.

Now, why is the second program more efficient than the first, since they both do the same thing? The answer lies in the use of memory or rather in the lack of memory use in the second program. The first example declares a char array with five elements. This means that 5 bytes must be set aside for exclusive storage to this array. Next, a string constant is used that also requires 5 storage bytes. The "contents" of the constant are copied to the array elements. Once this procedure is complete, there are two separate strings containing "DATA" residing in program memory, a total of 10 bytes for program string data.

In the second example using the char pointer, we still have the string constant, requiring 5 bytes of storage. But we do not have to reserve another 5 bytes of storage for an array to which this constant can be copied. There is no char array. Therefore, the string data storage requirements of this program are half that of the previous program. Of course, the pointer, itself, requires 2 bytes of storage, but this still leaves a savings of 3 bytes over the previous program.

Big deal! A lousy 3 bytes! So what? These are good observations, but percentages will be more revealing. The latter program was 30 percent more efficient from the standpoint of string data storage. If we were dealing with 1000 strings, a 30 percent savings is nothing to turn your back on. This is sometimes difficult to comprehend when such simple program examples are used for demonstration purposes. Just remember that C programs may require hundreds, thousands, or hundreds of thousands of storage bytes, depending on the scope and complexity of a particular program. Any savings of memory, in these situations, may be essential.

There is one other area of efficiency in which the latter program excels. There is no **strcpy()** function as in the first example. This function is unnecessary, because no copy of the constant is made. The pointer is directed to the memory location of the constant. Since the function does not have to be invoked, the storage required for its source code is not a part of the executable program. More memory space is spared. Plus, the execution time required by the **strcpy()** function is saved. The end result is that the latter program executes faster and requires considerably less memory space. This is a sizable savings that will multiply by the complexity of any programs that require similar programming structures.

Using the Turbo C compiler in small-memory mode and optimizing for size, the first program, using a char array, resulted in an object code size of 265 bytes compared with 237 bytes for the pointer version. When C is run under MS-DOS, there is always a high overhead, this being the operating system interface that allows a C program to be supported and executed. The executable (.EXE) files for these two programs measure out at 5778 and 5730 bytes, respectively, with the pointer version being the smaller of the two. This represents approximately 11 percent memory savings regarding the object code and only 1 percent savings in source code size for the pointer version. However, as a C program builds in complexity, the overhead tends to remain at relatively the same size. A much greater savings would be had if many, many operations were to be carried out when comparing the pointer version to the char array example.

It must be understood that an expression of:

```
*(a + 3)
```

in no way changes the value of the address in a. Rather, it simply uses this initial address as a reference point, adding a value of 3 to it in order to access a particular character. However, there is a slightly simpler method of accomplishing the same thing the previous programs did while saving a bit more storage space. The following program demonstrates this method:

```
main()
{

        char *a;

        a = "DATA";

        while (*a != '\0')
                printf("%c\n", *a++);

}
```

Such an alteration reduces our object code to 233 bytes. This method actually changes the value of the pointer. Within the **while** loop an exit clause of

```
*a != '\0'
```

is used. This simply states that the loop is to continue cycling until the character returned by `*a` is the NULL, which is represented in standard C terminology as `'\0'`. This is the character equivalent of numeric 0 (zero). Within the **printf()** function, there is the expression

```
*a++
```

This is the standard usage of the incremental operator, which may be used either in front of or following the variable name. When the incremental operator precedes the variable name, the variable value (memory address in this instance) is incremented and then the object value is returned. When it follows the variable name, the object value is returned, then the address is incremented. The latter operation is what is desired in this program. Each time **printf()** is executed within the loop, the current object value or character is returned by `*a`; then the memory address in `a` is incremented by 1. If we assume that `"DATA"` resides at 158, then the `'D'` is located at this address. After the `'D'` is returned within **printf()**, the address contained in the pointer is incremented by 1. On the next pass of the loop, `a` is pointing to 159. The `'A'` is returned to **printf()** and the address is incremented again. This continues until the NULL character is read, signaling the end of the string. The loop starts to cycle again, but the exit clause is satisfied. `*a` is now equal to `'\0'`, and the loop terminates.

Notice that the method of stepping the value of the pointer eliminates the need for the int variable used in preceding programs. This saves storage space. Again, the amount in these examples is negligible, but in larger programs, the savings that can be had by this type of programming can make a very large difference.

There is an even more compact way of performing the same operation carried out by the previous program examples:

```
main()
{

        char *a;

        a = "DATA";

        while (*a)
                printf("%c\n", *a++);

}
```

Now, this program does not save any additional storage space when compared to the previous example, but it is quicker to write, as all extraneous source coding is eliminated. The change occurs in the escape clause within the **while** loop. This notation may seem strange, but that's part of the beauty (and the cause of headaches for beginners) of the C language syntax.

The escape clause within the **while** loop is merely a conditional test. The clause:

```
*a != '\0'
```

returns a value other than zero as long as the character in `*a` is not equal to numeric zero. Again, the character `'\0'` and the number 0 (zero) are one and the same. So, the **while** statement is going to continue looping as long as its escape clause does not equate to zero. When `*a` does equal zero, the clause also equates to zero. Since the clause equates to zero, the escape condition is met and **while** terminates its loop. Understand that, in this example, the fact that the clause returns a zero when `*a` returns a zero is just a coincidence. If the escape clause in **while** had read:

```
while (*a != 65)
```

then the clause would equate to zero when the first `'A'` in `"DATA"` was returned. (`'A'` is equal to ASCII 65.) The clause equates to zero because the conditional test is not met. This condition states that *a is not equal to 65. The clause returns a "true" value of other than zero as long as the condition of the test is met. However, when *a is indeed equal to 65, the condition is no longer met, and a "false" value or zero is returned. However, when handling string quantities, we are always checking for the end of the string, which is numeric zero. We can use this to advantage when writing C programs that access strings. This is exactly what has been done with our last program example.

We know that the last character in a string is '\0' or numeric zero. So, instead of going to the trouble of writing an escape sequence that evaluates the return value of a clause, let's simply evaluate the true value of the pointer object. Therefore, **while** evaluates the content of *a. As long as this value is not zero, the loop continues to cycle. When the NULL character is read, the numeric value is zero and the loop is exited. Again, **while** will continue to cycle as long as it evaluates a value other than zero. The zero signals termination.

It is important to remember that these last examples have incremented the address stored in the pointer. When the loop is exited, the pointer no longer has the address of the start of the constant. Rather, it contains the address of the NULL character at the end of the string constant. This can be proven by the following program:

```
main()
{

        char *a;

        a = "DATA";

        printf("%u\n", a);

        while (*a)
                printf("%c\n", *a++);

        printf("%u\n", a);

}
```

On my machine, this program will display:

```
158
D
A
T
A
162
```

The breakdown on storage of the string constant is as follows:

```
 D   A   T   A  \0
158 159 160 161 162
```

This proves the point. The pointer that was initially given the address of 158 now contains an address value of 162. The latter value is where the NULL character is stored. Programmers must remember that when the address value in a pointer is incremented, the initial address is changed just as it is when, say, the value in an int variable is incremented.

This condition makes no difference to this program since it terminates right after the loop is exited. Also, when a pointer is handed as an argument to a function, the variable that represents this function argument is not the same pointer that was handed to the function. Rather, it is another declared pointer that contains the same address that the function argument pointer did. The pointer that is incremented from within a function does change memory address value. However, this in no way changes the address value of the pointer from the calling program. Remember, arguments are passed to functions by value. A pointer passes the value of the address it contains. This value is assigned to the pointer declared within the function. Any changes in the initial value passed to the function are in effect only within the function proper. Values passed from calling programs are never altered. This applies to pointers as well as to auto variables. However, when a function has a memory address, it can write changes to that address. The following program will explain this further:

```
main()
{

        char *a;

        a = "DATA";

        printf("%u\n", a);

        vert(a);

        printf("%u\n", a);

}
vert(p)
char *p;
{

        while (*p)
                printf("%c\n", *p++);

}
```

On the test machine, this program displays:

```
158
D
A
T
A
158
```

This means that "DATA" is stored at relative memory address 158 and that a points to this address before entering the **vert()** function. The address in a is passed to this function as a value that is then assigned as the memory address of p, the char pointer that is declared within the function. The print operation takes place from within the function by incrementing the address value of p. When the function is exited, p contains the address value of 162, the NULL character position in the constant's storage area. However, the address value in a, the argument pointer, remains unchanged. The main point here is that a is not passed to the function! The memory address value in a is passed . . . again, as a value. The memory address is that of "DATA" and that location is accessed by p, which initially points to the same thing a points to.

Problems

It's not uncommon to see a program similar to the following:

```
main()
{

        char *a;

        strcpy(a, "DATA");

        printf("%s\n", a);

}
```

This is totally and absolutely wrong. To what does a point? You don't know the answer to that question, and neither do I. This is a prime example of overwriting memory. When char *a is declared, it points to a random location in memory. In typical computer jargon, we can say that a points to garbage as soon as it is declared. However, one person's garbage may be another person's treasure. The same applies here. One program function's garbage may be another program function's meat and potatoes. As was stated in prior chapters, when you overwrite computer memory, you're involved in a game of logic Russian roulette and the outcome can be almost anything. The program may work or seem to work perfectly. If this is true, then the hammer fell on an empty chamber. The computer could lock up or, worse, return inaccurate information. Bingo! The hammer fell on a loaded chamber. While such occurrences rarely bring about disaster when using small-memory-model compilers, large-memory models may allow a memory overwrite to trip a few interrupts and, maybe, erase the file control block on your hard-disk drive. Bingo again! You've just rendered your entire hard disk useless!

Another common and absolutely wrong use of a char pointer is demonstrated in the following program:

```
main()
{

        char *a;

        gets(a);

        printf("%s\n", a);

}
```

Here again is the notorious memory overwrite. The **gets()** function retrieves characters from the keyboard and stores them in memory. The keyword here is "store." Store means that there must be room to put something somewhere. Where in memory are the keyboard characters to be put? The answer is in the series of memory locations pointed to by `a`. Where does `a` point? Anywhere!

A pointer must *always* be given a memory address! This applies in every case. The address can be specified directly, as a numeric value or, as is more often the case, indirectly by assigning the declared pointer the address of a variable or other program object.

Anytime an attempt is made to "copy" something to a pointer, a mistake is being made. A pointer can only be assigned a memory value. This breaks down into a practice of "the pointer equals this," "this" being an address.

All of the previous incorrect examples of pointer usage tried to "copy" bytes of data into memory locations that were unknown. The proper type of variable to be used for copying char string data is a char array, sized to meet the maximum string input from the keyboard. It's important to remember that once a char pointer is given the address of a char array, the pointer points to a "safe" area of memory for storage of up to the maximum amount of characters specified in the array subscript. The following program will demonstrate this concept:

```
main()
{
        char a[40], *p;

        p = a;

        gets(p);

        printf("%s   %s\n", p, a);

}
```

This program will accept a keyboard input of up to 39 characters safely. That is, the array can hold 40 bytes without overwriting memory. The pointer, p, is given the address of the array. This means that it points to 40 safe bytes of memory. When this program is executed, a keyboard input of:

```
COMPUTER <Return>
```

will result in:

```
COMPUTER  COMPUTER
```

written to the display screen. This occurs because the pointer serves as the argument to **gets()**. The bytes input at the keyboard are written to the storage area to which p points. Since this is the area allocated for char array a, the string is copied into a. Both a and p will return the same character string to **printf()**.

Of course, the program would be more efficient without the pointer (in this particular example) and could best be written as:

```
main()
{

        char a[40];

        gets(a);

        printf("%s  %s\n", a, a);

}
```

This example writes the same information to the screen, and works in exactly the same way, since in the previous example, both p and a pointed to the same memory location.

Can you deduce what the following program will display on the monitor screen?

```
main()
{

        char a[40], *p;

        strcpy(a, "SILICON");

        p = a;

        strcpy(a, "CONTROL");

        printf("%s\n", p);

}
```

If you answered "SILICON", then you are totally incorrect. The correct answer is "CONTROL". Remember, the pointer, p, was given the address of the array. It was not made to point to either of the two string constants, only to the start of the array. When p is assigned the address of a, the pointer immediately points to the first string copied into a. The bytes that make up "SILICON" were stored in a at the time of this initial assignment. However, the next program operation copies a new string into a. "CONTROL" overwrites "SILICON". The pointer still points to the memory address of a; therefore, p now points to "CONTROL", which resides at the same location previously used to store "SILICON".

When a pointer points to the address of an array, this means that the pointer is completely interchangeable with the array as far as arguments to functions such as **printf()** are concerned. Some would say that p is equal to anything a is equal to. This is correct but can also be misleading. Since both p and a are pointers (remember, the array name becomes a pointer when used without the subscripting brackets), they both contain the same memory address. It is more accurate to say that when a declared pointer is given the address of an array, the contents of the array and the string contents that the pointer accesses are always the same.

There is a difference, a big one, in a variable being equal to a value and in one being the *same* as that value. The following program demonstrates this difference:

```
main()
{

        char a[40], *p;

        strcpy(a, "GARAGE");

        p = "HOUSE";

}
```

Hopefully, this will clear up any misconceptions surrounding the terms "equal to" and "same as." Here, the string constant, "GARAGE", is copied into the char array. From an earlier discussion, we know that this causes the bytes that make up the constant to be copied or reproduced in the array. When this copy operation is complete, there are two strings in memory. The first is the constant, "GARAGE". The second is the copy of the constant, also "GARAGE". Therefore, the contents of the array are equal to

"GARAGE", but they are not the same as the constant, "GARAGE". The constant resides at one memory location; the contents of the array, at another.

On the other hand, the pointer is assigned the memory address of the constant, "HOUSE". No copy takes place. "HOUSE" is found only once in program memory. Therefore, p points to "HOUSE", the constant. What p points to is the constant itself. In this regard, they are one and the same. The address of "HOUSE" and the address to which p points are the same.

In human terms, we can compare this example with identical twins. They look alike. You can't tell the difference between the two when they stand side by side. However, there are two of them. They are not one and the same. In the above example, "GARAGE" was twinned. By the same token, "HOUSE" is an individual. Only one exists. Therefore, anything that equates to "HOUSE" is "HOUSE" and not a copy.

Arrays of Pointers

To this point in the discussion, we have compared char arrays to char pointers. An array is a collection of single data units, while a pointer, as always, is a special variable that holds the address of a memory location. However, arrays of pointers are not only possible but practical as well. The following program will start this portion of the discussion:

```
main()
{

        char a[5][15];
        int x;

        strcpy(a[0], "DATA");
        strcpy(a[1], "LOGIC");
        strcpy(a[2], "MICROPROCESSOR");
        strcpy(a[3], "COMPUTER");
        strcpy(a[4], "DISKETTE");
```

```
        for (x = 0; x < 5; ++x)
            printf("%s\n", a[x]);

}
```

This program simply copies five string constants to the two-dimensional array, `a`. In making the declaration, the second portion of the subscript determines maximum string length. Since it is known that `"MICROPROCESSOR"` will be the longest string and that it contains 14 characters, then the minimum string length declared for the array is 15 characters or bytes. This will be just large enough to contain the 14 characters in `"MICROPROCESSOR"` plus one more (15 total) for the NULL character.

The multidimensional array can also be classified as an array of strings or even as an array of char arrays. In any event, the array declaration does not allow for the dimensioning for different string lengths. If the maximum string length is 15, then storage of this quantity is provided for all five of the string elements. This applies even though most of the strings are less than eight characters in length. Since 15 bytes are provided for each string, there is an obvious waste of storage.

The **strcpy()** function is used to make a copy of the string constants and store each in the bytes provided for each string in the array.

Finally, a **for** loop is entered, which causes the contents of the array to be written to the screen. This is a multidimensional array, so the expression `a[x]` is a pointer to the `x` element or `x` string in the array. This may seem to conflict with earlier discussions where it was stated that the array variable name without the subscript brackets was a pointer, while the array name with brackets returned the object. This applies only to single-dimension arrays. With two dimensions, a single set of brackets with the name is a pointer, while a construct of:

```
a[x][y]
```

returns the object at the array position specified by the values of `x` and `y`. Therefore, the expression:

```
a[0]
```

where a is a multidimensional array, is a pointer to the first element of the first string in the array. a[1] is a pointer to the first element of the second string, and so on.

In addition to the wasted memory usurped by the array, which must size all string elements to the length of the maximum expected string, there is the fact that storage is required for constants as well as for copies of those constants. This is a most unsatisfactory condition and should be remedied, if possible. Pointers make this a distinct and easily accomplished possibility, as is demonstrated by the following program:

```
main()
{

        char *p[5];
        int x;

        p[0] = "DATA";
        p[1] = "LOGIC";
        p[2] = "MICROPROCESSOR";
        p[3] = "COMPUTER";
        p[4] = "DISKETTE";

        for (x = 0; x < 5; ++x)
                printf("%s\n", p[x]);

}
```

This program declares an array of char pointers. The designation

```
char *p[5];
```

declares p to be an array of five char pointers. The pointer to the first string is a[0], the second string a[1], the third a[2], and so on. As always, nothing is copied to a pointer. Rather, it is assigned a memory address. In this case, each of the five pointers in the array is assigned the address of a constant. This avoids the copying procedure from the previous program and also the doubled storage requirements. The rest of the program is handled in a fashion that is identical to the previous example. The program run appears to be identical with the one that used the multidimensional char array.

However, from a memory usage standpoint, this program is very different. Using the Turbo C compiler on the test computer, the multidimensional char array version consumed 409 bytes in object code format and 5880 bytes as an executable file. The pointer version of this same program required only 331 bytes for the object code and 5800 for the executable file. This means a 23 percent savings in code size for the object module and about 1.5 percent decrease in executable code. This is still not highly significant, but the percentages of savings will grow as program complexity increases, especially in regard to the storage of objects.

Summary

The use of C language pointers of type char is the most common of all. It can be seen that char pointers are closely aligned with char arrays, and the two can be used interchangeably in many applications. At the same time, there are still very large differences in the two, mostly regarding storage techniques. Like all variables, char arrays are allocated storage space based on the subscript value specified by the programmer. Char arrays are used to "store" data. However, like all pointers, those of type char are allocated no storage areas for common objects (in this case, char data). The only thing a char pointer can store is a memory address.

On declaration, a char pointer holds the address of a random memory location. This uninitialized address value should be considered "garbage," useless for any practical programming purpose.

It is only when the char pointer is "assigned" an address that it becomes initialized. It then points to a place in memory, again, specified directly or indirectly by the programmer.

Any variable, pointer types included, is useless and dangerous when it contains an unprogrammed value. It is always necessary to give the pointer something to point to. False assumptions about where a pointer points can lead to, at minimum, a faulty program that is very difficult to debug. In a worst-case scenario, data may be written to a "protected" memory location, creating havoc with the operating system interfaces and possibly resulting in a permanent loss of stored data.

A char pointer expects to point to a memory location allocated to store data of type char. This means 1 byte of storage for one character in most MS-DOS systems. Char pointers are often used as an efficient means of manipulating string constants. They may also access the storage areas of char arrays. In the latter usage, they may be treated just like the array. The important concept here is that the char pointer always contains the memory address of a safe area of memory, one designed for char or char string operations.

The uses outlined in this chapter are certainly not the full extent of operations for char pointers. Pointers of this type are especially suited to other operations, mainly because their largest storage units consist of data that can be contained in a single byte of memory.

Chapter 6

Pointers and Memory Access

Since pointers have the ability to point to different areas of memory and to read and write information at these points, it would seem obvious that they would be the ideal instruments for performing manipulations in and to memory. Every computer language contains some mechanism that will allow any memory location to be specified for the purposes of returning the byte contents from that location or to alter the same byte. Such mechanisms are usually referred to as "peek/poke" devices.

All of the discussions that have been offered to this point have used program examples that were compiled using the small-memory-model version of the Turbo C compiler. This model restricts memory access to a 64K data segment unless special "far" pointers or functions are used. This chapter will explore large-memory-model versions of the Turbo C compiler as well as "far" pointers. However, the start of this discussion still uses the small-memory model, as it is adequate for introductory purposes.

The following program is a partial repeat of several others from the previous chapter, but it will be examined in a different light:

```
main()
{
        char *a;

        a = "ANGULAR";

        printf("%d\n", *a);

}
```

Note that the **printf()** function uses a conversion specification of `%d` instead of `%c`. The latter would display the value in `*a` as a character. The `%d` specification causes this same value to be displayed as an integer. The value displayed on the screen will be 65, the ASCII code for `'A'`.

We know that pointer `a` is given the address of the constant in the

```
a = "ANGULAR";
```

assignment line. Let's assume for the purposes of this discussion that the storage for the constant begins at address 158 in the 64K segment. What has this program done?

The answer is that it has "peeked" at memory location 158 in the segment. The byte value at this address is 65. This clearly demonstrates that all a peek consists of is returning the byte value from a specified memory location.

The original C programming language contained a **peek()** function, and all popular versions contain similar functions in various forms and under the guise of various names. However, a peek function in C is rather redundant, since pointers allow for such easy access to this operation by direct programming methods.

The following program will demonstrate a "poke" operation:

```
main()
{

        char *a;

        a = "ANGULAR";

        *a = 66;

        printf("%s\n", a);

}
```

When this program is executed, it will display

```
BANGULAR
```

on the screen. The assignment

```
*a = 66;
```

causes the byte pointed to by `a` to be replaced with the assignment to `*a`. Remember, the unary `*` operator causes the specific byte to be returned or, in this case, written by assignment. What has occurred here is a typical "poke" operation. Pointer `a` points to the memory address where the constant is written, specifically, to the first byte in the string at location 158. `*a` returns this byte or can be used to write another byte on top of it. In this case the new byte has a value of 66 and is poked into memory over top of the initial value of 65. ASCII 65 is the letter `'A'` and ASCII 66 is the letter `'B'`. Memory has been altered by this poke operation. The **printf()** function is used to display the result of the change made in memory; thus "BANGULAR" is displayed.

Memory Models

Throughout this text, references have been made to the various memory models available in the Borland Turbo C Compiler used as the reference compiler for this book. Turbo C, along with most other popular C compilers for MS-DOS machines, offers several categories of compilers. These can be classified into two basic models: small- and large-memory models. Technically, Turbo C offers "tiny," "small," and "compact" models, each of which falls into the overall classification of "small-memory models." Large-memory models are broken down into "medium," "large," and "huge." For our discussion, the main difference between these two classes is in the default size of the pointers they directly support. The small-memory model, which has been used for all programming examples to this point in the discussions has 2-byte pointers, while large-memory models offer 4-byte pointers.

From an execution efficiency standpoint, the small-memory model offers the fastest execution speed and code size. However, the small-memory model also limits its pointers to 2-byte entities. A 2-byte pointer contains the same storage capacity of an unsigned integer. (*Note:* Byte size for various types of data may vary on different types of computers. Most, if not all, MS-DOS C implementations utilize the same storage parameters as does the Turbo C compiler, i.e., 1 byte for chars, 2 bytes for ints and unsigned numbers, 4 bytes for floats and long integers, and 8 bytes for double-precision floating-point values.)

An unsigned integer can represent a maximum value of 65536. Any pointer that is declared in the normal fashion using a small-memory-model compiler is allocated 2 bytes for address storage. This applies regardless of the type of pointer that is declared. Since only 2 bytes of storage are allocated, this means that the maximum memory address value can be only 65536. This severely limits the memory that can be addressed, as a typical system may have addresses spreading out to 10 times this amount or more.

Early C compilers for MS-DOS machines were available in the small-memory model only. Most made no provisions for memory excursions outside of the 64K data segment. Later versions offered special functions that would address any valid memory location. Even newer compilers were offered in large- and small-memory models. The newest, of which Turbo C is a part, also allows for the use of special 4-byte pointers to be specifically declared from within small-memory models. A programmer who wants the fastest possible execution speed will usually try to stay within the confines of the small-memory compiler versions. Prior to the newest type of compiler, the need to "rove" around in all of a computer's memory forced the use of the large-memory models and their slower execution speeds and large code sizes. Today, it is possible to use a small-memory model and resort to 4-byte or "far" pointers when memory excursions outside of the 64K data segment are desired.

For specific peek/poke operations, most modern C compilers also offer functions that address these. In Turbo C, these are called **peekb()** and **pokeb()**. The first returns a single byte from memory based on segment and offset arguments. The second writes a single byte to memory based on the same arguments plus the byte value to be written. This allows for the peek/poke "standard" form of addressing users of the Microsoft BASIC Interpreter have become so accustomed to. For instance, if we wish to write directly to the monochrome screen in BASIC, the following program might be used:

```
10 DEF SEG = &HB000
20 POKE 0, 67
```

This will cause the letter 'C' to be written in the upper left-hand corner of the screen. Since BASIC works in a manner similar to a small C compiler version, only one 64K area of memory can be accessed at a time. The DEF SEG statement allows the address of any 64K segment to be defined. The POKE statement can access any of 65,536 bytes in this segment. We can move through all of memory with this combination, since if we need to go outside of the specified 64K segment, we simply change the DEF SEG value. In the above example, &HB000 is the address of the monochrome screen buffer specified in hexadecimal format as is customary. This HEX value is the equivalent of 45046 decimal. Programmers who are using the color graphics adapter would specify an address of &HB800 (47104 decimal), which is the start of the color screen buffer. The POKE statement's first argument is the offset into the segment. In this case the offset is zero, which specifies the first byte at &HB000. The second argument is the byte to be written to the specified memory location. ASCII 67 is the letter 'C'.

In Turbo C, the **pokeb()** function allows for the same type of addressing as was demonstrated by the previous BASIC program.

To accomplish the same thing in Turbo C using the small-memory model, the following program can be used:

```
main()
{

        pokeb(0xb000, 0, 67);

}
```

Here, the DEF SEG value from the previous BASIC program serves as the first argument to the function. The second argument is the offset into the segment, and the third argument is the byte value to be written. The &H designation in BASIC means that the number to follow is in hexadecimal format. The hexadecimal format is indicated differently in C language using the 0x (zero-x) designation.

However, it seems rather wasteful to use a function to perform this simple operation, especially since we already know that pointers can address any area of memory when a program is compiled using a large-memory-model compiler. The following program must be compiled using the large-memory model of the Turbo C compiler:

```
main()
{

        char *a;

        a = (char *) 0xb0000000;

        *a = 67;

}
```

That's all there is to it. No function has to be invoked that will result in slower execution. The poke is handled directly by the char pointer. The only unusual feature of this program to some readers will be the address value. One must remember that far pointers, the type created when any pointer is declared using a large-memory-model compiler, are 4-byte entities. With 8 bits to a byte, we can say that 2-byte pointers require 16-bit numbers and 4-byte pointers must have 32-bit addresses. This is what the latter is, a 32-bit address specifically naming the monochrome screen buffer segment of memory in absolute terms. In 8-bit terms, we can break the 32-bit address down into a segment and an offset as in:

```
                SEG        OFFSET

0x              b000       0000
```

If you are accustomed to providing addresses in 8-bit values, and most users of MS-DOS machines and software are, then simply follow the hexadecimal value with four zeros. Mathematically, the conversion method involves multiplying the 8-bit address by `0x10000`. If you prefer to work within the decimal system (cumbersome when dealing with memory addresses), then multiply the decimal memory address by 65536 decimal.

In any event, the previous program must use absolute addressing when dealing with memory locations, and each address is given as a 32-bit (4-byte) quantity. `0xb0000000` is the address of the start of the monochrome display buffer. The assignment line uses a cast operator to coerce the numeric value to type `char *`. This is necessary in type-casting the numeric value to a form that is acceptable to the pointer.

Once the assignment of a memory address has been made, we know that `a` points to the start of, in this case, the monochrome screen buffer. This means that `*a` will access the object value stored in the byte at this location. Therefore, a construct of:

```
*a = 67;
```

reassigns a value of 67 to this byte. The letter `'C'`, which is represented by decimal 67, appears in the upper left corner of the screen. This is far more efficient from both a programming and an execution speed standpoint when compared to calling the **pokeb()**

function. Calling a function from a program requires additional execution time and larger code size.

When a C program calls a function, the calling program actually relinquishes control to the function. This takes more time than if the function were actually written within the calling program, proper. You can literally see the difference calling a function like **pokeb()** makes in execution speed. The following program represents a method of filling the monochrome screen with `'C'` characters using **pokeb()**:

```
main()
{

        int x;

        for (x = 0; x <= 3999; x += 2)
            pokeb(0xb000, x, 67);

}
```

This program must be compiled under the large-memory-model compiler option offered in Turbo C. This is necessary for comparison purposes with the program that is to follow. Before moving on to the comparison program, let's discuss a few traits of this one.

The monochrome screen is composed of 4000 single bytes. Each even-number byte (including 0) will display a character on the screen when "poked" with an ASCII value. In this case it is 67 for the letter `'C'`. However, each odd-number byte (1 to 3999) is called an "attribute" byte. The standard screen fills each attribute byte with a value of 7, as this will bring about normal display of each character. Other attribute values will cause the preceding character to be displayed in flashing, bold, or underlined format. Since the screen attribute bytes already contain a value of 7 for normal display, it is unnecessary to address the odd bytes at all in this program example.

The **for** loop steps variable `x` from a value of 0 (zero) to 3999 in increments of 2. On the first pass of the loop, `x` is equal to 0. On the next pass, it will be equal to 2, then to 4, then 6, etc. This means that only the even-number bytes will be accessed. These are the bytes to which character ASCII codes are to be written.

The **pokeb()** function is called on each pass of the loop. Note that the segment value is always `0xb000`, the 8-bit code for the start of the screen buffer. (*Note:* If you are using a graphics display adapter, this value should be changed to `0xb800`.) The **pokeb()** function requires an 8-bit address, even when it is compiled by the large-memory-model compiler option. The stepping value of **x** is used as the offset argument, while 67 is the byte to be poked into all accessed locations.

On the first pass of the loop, 67 will be poked into byte `0xb000 + 0`. On the next pass, the byte location is `0xb000 + 2`, then `0xb000 + 4`, etc. When the loop times out, all of the character bytes in the screen buffer will be filled with the `'C'` character.

You will see these characters written very rapidly to the monitor screen. Those readers with ultrafast computer clocks should try to toggle machine speed to the lowest setting, if possible, in order for the time differences between this and the next program to be appreciated.

On a standard 4.77-mHz IBM PC, the characters are written in just a moment, but you can actually see each line being formed in the process of this write.

Again, this program calls a function that, in turn, declares additional variables, executes its code, and then returns control to the calling program. When the loop recycles, the function is called again, and the process is continued until the loop times out.

The next program does exactly the same thing (on-screen) as the former example, but it calls no function. Rather, it programs a pointer to do the poke operation:

```
main()

{
        char *a;
        int x;

        a = (char *) 0xb0000000;
```

```
        for (x = 0; x <= 3999; x += 2)
                *(a + x) = 67;

}
```

Compile this program using the large-memory-model option as before. When it is executed, the monitor will be filled with a full screen of characters (seemingly) instantaneously. This method of poking in characters is much faster. The reason for this lies in the fact that no function was called. For all intents and purposes, the **pokeb()** function works along the same principles that this program incorporates. With functions, however, there is a much higher overhead in that they must declare additional variables that this latter program didn't require.

Newcomers to C language often become confused over the avant-garde use of characters such as `'C'`, `'f'`, and `'L'`, interchanging them with numbers. C language makes no distinction whatsoever between `'A'` and the numeric value 65. They are both one and the same. Certainly, functions are available that will display 65 as `'A'` or vice versa. The simple integer assignment:

```
x = 66;
```

may also be written as:

```
x = 'B';
```

They both mean exactly the same thing. In both cases, variable `x` was assigned a value of 66 decimal. How this value is displayed on the screen depends on the conversion specification given to **printf()**, assuming that this is the function used for display. A conversion specification of `%c` will cause a numeric value argument of 66 to be displayed as the letter `'B'`. If the conversion specification is `%d`, then the same value will be displayed as decimal 66. If you go in for hexadecimal numbers, then a specification of `%x` will cause decimal 66 to be displayed as `HEX 42`. Similarly, a specification of `%o` will cause 66 to be displayed as `Octal 102`. All of these values, 66D, 'B', 42H, and 102-OCT are equal. How they are displayed on the screen is up to the programmer.

Now that the "mysteries" of poking bytes into memory has been explained, let's concentrate on peek operations. The process is the same in that memory locations are accessed. However, instead of writing a byte of data to such a location, the byte already in that location is read. The following program demonstrates this operation using the turbo C **peekb()** function:

```
main()
{

        int x;

        x = peekb(0xb000, 0);

        printf("%d\n", x);

}
```

The function allows the segment to be input as an 8-bit quantity, while its second argument is the offset (number of bytes) into that segment. This function returns a value of type int. The returned value is the object value of the byte specified. Again, the segment address is the start of the monochrome-display buffer. Therefore, if the letter 'A' appears in the upper left corner of the screen prior to running this program, x will be equal to 65, the decimal equivalent of character 'A'.

The following program shows a more efficient method of accomplishing the same thing by directly programming a pointer to handle the access:

```
main()
{

        char *a;

        a = (char *) 0xb0000000;
```

```
        printf("%d\n", *a);

}
```

This program must be compiled under the large-memory-model option of the Turbo C compiler. As with the equivalent example of a poke operation, this program declares `a` to be a pointer of type `char`. This pointer is then given the address of the screen buffer in 32-bit format. Now, instead of assigning a value to `*a`, we simply print the value already in `*a`. The returned byte is displayed as an integer value, although it could also be displayed as a character, a hexadecimal value, or even an octal number if desired. What is returned by `*a` is a single value. How it is displayed is up to you.

How would you go about writing your own function to handle a peek operation? True, the direct method is most efficient, but if you had to write such a function for some unknown purpose, you would simply follow the program logic presented above and end up with:

```
int peeker(loc)
long loc;
{

        char *mem;

        mem = (char *) loc;

        return(*mem);

}
```

That's all there is to it. Of course, this assumes that the address handed to the function (represented here by `loc`) would be a 32-bit quantity, and that this function would be used only in programs compiled under large-memory models. A long int-type argument is handed to this function, since this variable's storage capabilities are adequate to handle full-memory addressing. A char pointer is declared within the function and is assigned the value in `loc` as an address. Once our pointer is pointing to the right location, all that is necessary is to return the byte.

Oh! You want a small-memory version as well? That's fairly simple too, but first it is necessary to go into a little more detail about the features offered in Turbo C and most modern C compilers.

The advantage of the small-memory-model options in most C compilers lies in the fact that 2-byte pointers are used, which facilitates execution speed and allows for smaller code size. The disadvantage of this same model is that the same 2-byte pointers cannot be used to access all memory locations, so you are stuck with resorting to functions that will address memory for you and the slower execution speeds that are incurred through their use.

The advantage of the large-memory-model options of the same compilers is that the 4-byte pointers give full access to all memory addresses. However, using large-memory models will result in slower equivalent execution times and larger code.

One solution is to use a small-memory-model compiler that offers the option of declaring 4-byte pointers. This is exactly what the best C compilers do today. The small-memory models may be used in the standard way and will provide compact code and the fastest execution speed. All pointers declared in the normal fashion will be 2-byte types. However, if you need a special pointer to access a memory location outside of the code area restricted by the 2-byte entities, then all you need do is declare that special pointer.

Such pointers are declared by using the `far` keyword or modifier. The following program is compiled using a small-memory-model option and illustrates the difference between "near" and "far" pointers:

```
main()
{

        char *a;
        char far *b;

        printf("%d   %d\n", sizeof(a), sizeof(b));

}
```

The first pointer, a, is declared using standard conventions and is allotted 2 bytes for storage. The second is modified by the far keyword and is a 4-byte entity. All of this assumes that the program is to be compiled under a small-memory-model option. The **printf()** function is used to display the size of each pointer in bytes using the standard C language **sizeof()** function. When the program is run, you will see that pointer a has a size of 2 bytes and b is sized at 4 bytes. Again, this program must be compiled using one of the small-memory-model options.

Now we have the best of both worlds: small-memory-model speed and economy; and the ability to declare far pointers to go anywhere in memory. Note that the declarations of these pointers were made on two separate program lines, but this was done for the sake of clarity. The standard method of making these two declarations would be in one line, such as:

```
char *a, far *b;
```

This declares a to be a standard pointer and b a far type, both of type char. Incidentally, the term *far* is quite appropriate and is based on assembly language nomenclature of near and far operations. The far pointer is able to gain access far away from the data segment into other memory areas. The standard, 2-byte pointer is known as a *near* type, since it must stay nearby, within a predetermined memory segment because of its 2-byte storage limitation.

The following program is the equivalent of the peek operation discussed earlier, but is compiled under one of the small-memory-model options:

```
main()
{

        char far *a;

        a = (char far *) 0xb0000000;

        printf("%d\n", *a);

}
```

That's all there is to it. You will notice that the cast operator contains the `far` modifier. You must remember that `a` is not a `char` pointer but a `char far` pointer. Notice also that the address is given as a 32-bit quantity as is required for 4-byte pointers. Other than the addition of `far`, the program is identical to a previous example and returns the first byte in the screen buffer as an integer.

Now, back to the problem that brought on this latest discussion in the first place. How does one write a peek function that can be compiled under a small-memory model and that will accept 8-bit addresses as the original Turbo C **peekb()** function does? It's easy using the far pointer option available. The function follows:

```
int peeker(seg, off)
int seg, off;
{

        char far *mem;

        mem = (char far *) (seg * 65536);
        return(*(mem + off));

}
```

Again, there's nothing to it! Our new function, called **peeker()** for lack of a better name, accepts two arguments. Both are of type `int`, the first being the 8-bit segment address while the second names the offset into memory.

The designation:

```
*(mem + off)
```

simply adds the offset value to the segment value and returns the byte at that address. This is directly in line with the operation of **peekb()**. BASIC programmers can think of `seg` as the `DEF SEG` value and `off` as the single argument they would pass to the **PEEK()** function in BASIC. Of course, we need to go from an 8-bit numeric quantity to the 32-bit equivalent, because `seg` is a far pointer. This is accomplished by simply multiplying the memory address in `seg` by 65536 decimal as this value is being assigned to the pointer. You could also state the multiplier value as `0x10000` to keep with the hexadecimal memory addressing convention.

Another method of writing this same function follows:

```
int peeker(seg, off)
int seg, off;
{

        char far *mem;

        mem = (char far *) (seg << 16) + off;

        return(*mem);

}
```

The (possibly) questionable line is:

```
    mem = (char far *) (seg << 16) + off;
```

This is quite a mouthful, but it's easily explained. First of all:

```
            seg << 16
```

makes use of the left-shift operator in C language. This means exactly the same thing as multiplying `seg` by 65536. It requires less input typing, however, and is more expressive when dealing with hexadecimal values. After this operation takes place, the offset value is added on. Therefore, `mem` points to the proper address of `seg`, converted to a 32-bit address, plus `off`. This example is shown, because C programmers often use shortcuts that are not as clear as some of the simpler examples found in this text.

Of course, this function is superfluous, as we can accomplish the same thing without resorting to a function as has been amply demonstrated. The direct method will result in the most efficient program.

Why Char Pointers?

At this juncture in my seminars and C language workshops, someone invariably asks why char pointers are used for these purposes and not int or long types. That's a good question, and there is a good answer.

A char pointer expects a return value of type char or can be used to write a value of type char. (Remember, a char can be specified as the character itself as in `'C'` or as its ASCII code, 67. Both mean the same thing.) A char value is a 1-byte entity. On the other hand, int pointers expect an int return, which is a 2-byte value on MS-DOS systems. A long or float is a 4-byte entity, and a double is an 8-byte number. When we are peeking and poking around in memory, we normally wish to do this 1 byte at a time. Other pointer types will not allow for a 1-byte return or a 1-byte write, at least not in the direct way char pointers do.

"But you said all pointers in small-memory-model compilers for MS-DOS machines are 2-byte entities, and in large models, they have 4 bytes for storage!" That's right, but this applies only to the area set aside for the pointer to store an address! The number of bytes they return or access is fixed at 1 for chars, 2 for ints and unsigneds, 4 for floats and longs, and 8 for doubles.

The following program (compiled with a small-memory model) will help explain all of this:

```
main()
{

     int far *x;
     char far *a;

     x = (int far *) 0xb0000000;
     a = (char far *) 0xb0000000;

     system("cls");

     printf("%c\n\n\n", 'A');
```

```
        printf("%d\n%d\n", *a, *x);

}
```

This program declares two far pointers. Pointer x is of type int, while a is of type char. Both pointers are given the address of the start of the monochrome-display buffer. The **system()** function is used to call the MS-DOS "cls" command, which clears the display screen and resets the cursor to the upper left-hand corner. A **printf()** function is then called which prints an 'A' in the upper left corner of the screen followed by two carriage returns or newlines, as they are known in C terminology.

Another **printf()** function is used to display the values in *a and in *x. Remember, both of these pointers have been given the same address. Both point to the first byte of screen memory . . . but a is of type char and x is an int type.

The expectation here is that the final **printf()** line in the program would display two values of 65. But that's not what happens! Instead, you get 65 on one line and 1857 on the other. The char pointer returned the correct value, but so did the int pointer with its 1857. How can that be? There can't be two values for the first byte in the screen buffer! The latter is a true statement. However, the char pointer accesses memory in 1-byte quantities. A char can't represent more than one byte of data. On the other hand, the int pointer accesses data in 2-byte increments. The return from an int pointer is not a 1-byte quantity but a 2-byte value. Earlier, it was stated that the monochrome-screen buffer used every other byte (even numbers and zero) for character display. The odd bytes are used for character attribute values. In a normal screen, all of the odd bytes have a value of 7. Therefore, the value returned by the int pointer was the 2-byte combination of 65 and 7. The 65, as we already know, is the ASCII code for 'A'. The 7 is the attribute byte. The 2-byte coding for a numeric value of 1857 is, you guessed it, 65 and 7.

In short, the char pointer returned a 1-byte value that was written to the screen as its integer equivalent of 65. This is the only value found in that single byte. The int pointer returned a 2-byte standard int value that was also written to the screen as its 2-byte integer equivalent of 1857. This can also be explained mathematically as:

```
1857 % 256 = 65    \* First Byte *\
1857 \ 256 = 7     \* Second Byte *\
```

The opposite event takes place when a poke operation is attempted with a pointer of type int. Assuming that `x` is a far pointer to the start of the monochrome screen buffer and of type int, the expression:

```
*x = 65;
```

will cause a value of 65 (`'A'`) to be written to the first byte in the buffer, but a 0 (zero) will also be written at the second byte. The first write is what we're looking for. The second definitely is not! The second byte (the odd one) is the attribute byte for the screen display. A value of zero here causes the character at byte 1 to become invisible. The result for a full-screen write of all characters `'A'` is a blank screen if an int pointer is used for this purpose. You might think of pointers as returning one storage unit of data or of being used to write one storage unit of data. In fact, each accesses one storage unit in memory. This applies regardless of the type of pointer. However, the storage unit for a char type is 1 byte only. Storage unit size for all other data types is 2 bytes or more.

Far pointers specifically programmed from small-memory-model programs work just as well for writing or poking data into memory as well. The following program demonstrates a poke operation using a far pointer:

```
main()
{

        char far *a;

        a = (char far *) 0xb0000000;
```

```
        *a = 65;

}
```

This program writes an 'A' to the start of the screen buffer and can be compiled by the small-memory-model option. It should be stressed at this juncture that the large-memory-model classification of compiler options offers advantages other than being able to address all memory. These include the ability to handle large programs that will not compile using small-memory models. Of course, it is usually best to stay within the boundaries of the small-memory-model classifications wherever possible, but source code size and content will dictate the model that is best suited to a particular program. In some cases, you may have to try both model classifications (that is, those models that fall into the "small" category and those that fall into the "large") in order to see which compilation is best for a particular purpose. If you switch from one to the other, it will be necessary to change the source code slightly when pointer operations that use direct addresses are part of the code. For instance, if you compile a program under a large-memory model, then recompilation under a small-memory model will require that pointers used for far-memory access be redeclared far pointers. Going from a small- to a large-memory model is not nearly so tedious. In the large-memory models, a pointer is a 4-byte quantity by default. Any pointer that is declared far in the large-memory model is unaffected by the modifier, and is still allocated 4 bytes for address storage.

There are also other compiler options that are a combination of both large and small-memory models. For instance, the medium-memory model in Turbo C defaults to far pointers for the code (program) segment, but the data segment defaults to near pointers. This means that the medium-memory model is ideal for compiling C programs with a large amount of source code (larger than can be accommodated by the small-memory model) while still maintaining the efficiency of near pointers in the data segment. No far accesses into memory will be permitted without declaring far pointers for this purpose.

The opposite of this medium-memory model is called the "compact-memory model" in Turbo C. Here, the program segment is limited to near pointers, but all of memory can be accessed via the far-pointer default in the data segment. For C programs with only a moderate amount of source code, this model is ideal, especially if many excursions into far memory are anticipated.

Remember our "little man" from several chapters ago. The knapsack of the man who represents a char contains only a single compartment. When a pointer returns an object from a location, the entire contents of the knapsack are emptied. If you figure one item per compartment, then the little man who represents a char dumps only one item. The int little man dumps two, one from each compartment, the long int little man has four items, and so on. A similar thing happens when we try to fill those knapsacks. If you dump one item to a man with four compartments, the remaining three are also filled . . . with zeros, in this case. Those zeros may mean "nothing" when taken by themselves, but when they are part of an overall code, they mean much more.

Summary

A pointer stores the address of an object in memory. If the address is specified directly as a numeric memory location, the object at that address can be retrieved. This is a peek operation. If the address is assigned an object value, then the memory location is overwritten. This is a poke operation. Unintentional overwrites can be disastrous, but a poke is intentional and desirable (provided the programmer knows the ropes).

Char-type pointers are most desirable for reading and writing memory locations in this fashion. Their 1-byte objects are responsible for this desirability. All other types of pointers may also be used for memory accessing, but one must always remember the storage unit size of the various types.

Large-memory-model compilers automatically assign 4 bytes of address storage for all declared pointers. This allows excursions through all of a computer's memory (assuming typical maximum memory sizes). However, the large-memory-model compilers with their automatic "far" pointers create programs that are usually larger in size than those produced by small-memory-model compilers. Also, execution speed with large-memory-model compilations is slowed, sometimes considerably.

The Turbo C and most other high-quality compilers for MS-DOS machines now offer the advantage of declaring far pointers from within small-memory-model programs. This provides all-memory access while still maintaining the advantages of the small-memory-model attributes. It should be understood that, even with the small-memory models, 4-byte or far pointers still take longer to execute than do their 2-byte counterparts. However, small-memory-model programs that utilize both near (2-byte) and far pointers will execute faster than they would if compiled under a large-memory model where all pointers would be 4-byte types, regardless of their intended uses.

The old rule still applies. You should have seen in all of the program examples that pointers are always initialized, given a memory address *before* any reading or writing took place. When using far pointers, whether specifically declared from a small-memory-model program or from a large-memory-model program, the all-memory capability can lead to very real dangers if uninitialized pointers are used to write memory. With far pointers, it is now possible to tap into your system's various interrupts. An unintentional poke into memory can bring about some of the disasters alluded to earlier.

Always know where your pointers point!!!!

Chapter 7

Pointers and Memory Allocation Functions

The first rule of thumb when dealing with declared pointers is to give them something to point to. This is the pointer "initialization" process, and it cannot be repeated too often. All pointers must be assigned a memory address before usage, or they will address random memory locations that can literally wreck a program run or possibly even damage disk files.

In most previous program examples, pointers were assigned the memory addresses of other variables. In peek/poke operations, pointers were assigned the addresses of memory locations specifically for the purpose of reading a byte content or writing to a byte of storage.

There are many advantages in the use of pointers, but in most cases, standard variables are depended on for "safe" areas to which the pointers may point. Char arrays are necessary for storing "copied" strings, but they must be sized to accommodate the largest string length. Wouldn't it be nice if a device were available that would allow memory to be allocated based on the size of the string to be copied, rather than to some size roughly determined by the programmer and usually oversized for the sake of avoiding any possibility of an accidental memory overwrite?

Fortunately, C language offers such conveniences . . . if you know where to look.

Memory Allocation Functions

The two principal memory allocation functions that are a standard part of the C language function library are **malloc()** and **calloc().** They both perform the same basic function of setting aside a safe area of memory to which data may be written. These data blocks may be of any practical size. Both functions perform operations that check on memory availability, based on the memory block size requested. When a suitable block of memory is located, a pointer to the address of the allocated block is returned by the function. The main difference between **malloc()** and **calloc()** is that **calloc()** clears all of the allocated memory, poking zeros into each byte. **Malloc()** simply allocates the memory without clearing the bytes. The value of each byte is whatever random values were already contained in those memory locations.

Malloc()

The following program will begin our discussion of pointers and memory allocation functions. (*Note:* The next series of programs is intended for instruction purposes. Their operations will not display anything on the screen.)

```
main()
{

        char a[5][33];

        strcpy(a[0], "Happiness");
        strcpy(a[1], "Data");
        strcpy(a[2], "Now is the time for all good men");
```

```
        strcpy(a[3], "Forget");
        strcpy(a[4], "Computer");

}
```

This program uses a two-dimensional char array sized to hold a maximum of five strings, each with a maximum length of 33 bytes, including the NULL terminator. Similar to another example from an earlier portion of this text, we know that a could have been declared an array of char pointers in order to save on allocated memory. The above arrangement sets aside 165 bytes (5 * 33) for storage to the array. However, the total storage required for all of these five string constants is only 64 bytes. This means that 101 bytes are wasted in this particular example. The reason for the waste is the manner in which the array declaration must be made. The smallest value allowed in the second part of the subscript must be capable of containing the largest string. However, this large value applies to all of the other four string storage allocations within the array.

The following program is another example of possible wasted storage space:

```
main()
{

        int x;
        char a[5][256];

        for (x = 0; x < 5; ++x)
                gets(a[x]);

}
```

This example cannot use a pointer substitute, since no string constants are involved. The **gets()** function "copies" bytes retrieved from the keyboard into memory. This program assumes that the longest string will be composed of 255 typed characters and makes room for the NULL with the last. There is no way of knowing just what will be input, so an overly large string length must be prepared for.

However, we can conserve memory allocation through the memory allocation functions and the addresses they return to pointers. The following program will allocate storage for the strings input at the keyboard, based on the length of each string:

```
main()
{

        char *a, b[256], *malloc();

        gets(b);

        a = malloc(strlen(b));

        strcpy(a, b);

}
```

The operation of this program is simple. Three `char` types are declared: `a` is a `char` pointer, `b` is a `char` array with a maximum storage of 256 characters including the NULL, and **malloc()** is declared a function that returns a `char` pointer. **Malloc()**, technically, returns a void and may be cast into returning a pointer of any legal type. In this exercise, it is declared a `char` pointer type.

The **get()** function uses char array `b` as its storage device. This array can accept up to 255 printable characters without overwriting memory. The last character is the NULL. Now, **malloc()** is called, and it uses the length of the string already contained in `b` and returned by the **strlen()** function to determine how many bytes must be allocated. The **strlen()** function returns the total number of bytes in the string, including the NULL. Therefore, **malloc()** will set aside just enough storage, no more—no less, to store the string in array `b`. Now, **strcpy()** is used to copy the string in `b` to the pointer location contained in `a`. This address was returned to `a` by the **malloc()** function.

Wait a minute! Didn't we just *copy* something to a pointer? Isn't this supposed to be taboo?

Ordinarily, the answer is "Yes." Nothing should be copied to an uninitialized pointer. However, this pointer has the address of a block in memory that has been allocated especially for storage. This is a safe area, as **malloc()** guarantees this. The **strcpy()** function treats `a` like it would a pointer to a char array. Before each copy, adequate storage is set aside at the address contained in `a`. If there is adequate storage, there is no reason why data cannot be copied into this block of memory. The argument to **malloc()** is the return from **strlen().** This ensures that the block is of adequate size. In other words, the address assignment returned by **malloc()** initializes the pointer.

This sample program is by no means complete but was simplified to bare essentials for explanation purposes. The use of memory allocation functions mandates checking their returns for a NULL.

The memory allocation functions will return NULL if the amount of memory is unavailable. If a null return is issued by the function, then the pointer value will be zero. If this test is not made and a NULL is returned, any attempt to write to the anticipated block of memory (which doesn't exist if the return is NULL) will result in a dangerous memory overwrite. The proper method of handling the operation carried out by the previous program is demonstrated by the following program:

```
#include <stdio.h>
main()
{

        char *a, b[256], *malloc();

        gets(b);

        a = malloc(strlen(b));

        if (a == NULL) {
```

```
                printf("Out of memory\n");
                exit(0);
        else
                strcpy(a, b);

    }
```

This can be shortened to:

```
#include <stdio.h>
main()
{

    char *a, b[256], *malloc;

    gets(b);

    if ((a = malloc(strlen(b))) == NULL) {
          printf("Out of memory\n");
          exit(0);
    }
    else
          strcpy(a, b);

}
```

In both of these examples, the return value from **malloc()** is tested for a value of NULL. The **stdio.h** header file is included with each program, as the definition of NULL is contained in this file. On most systems, NULL is a value of 0 (zero), but large-memory models require that the value be a long integer (0L). Therefore, you can skip inclusion of **stdio.h,** to avoid the extra memory required for storage of all of its definitions, by replacing it with:

```
#define NULL 0
```

for small-memory-model compilers or:

```
#define NULL 0L
```

for large-memory-model compilers.

When **malloc()** is called, a conditional test is conducted on the value returned to the pointer. If this value is NULL or zero, then the program displays an "Out of memory" prompt and terminates execution. If the value returned by **malloc()** is other than zero, then the allocation attempt was successful and this value becomes a pointer to the allocated block.

When large blocks of memory are necessary, the large-memory-model versions may be required, as the amount of available memory for allocation is not as limited as it is with the small-memory models.

Suppose, for some purpose or other, you wanted to create a char array that would hold a very, very large string, say, 60,000 characters. Don't try a declaration line like:

```
char a[60000];
```

as you'll quickly find out that this exceeds the size your compiler will accept. You may not be able to think of a reason why anyone would require an array of this size, but there are many. For instance, a whole block of characters, say, from a word-processor file, could be stored in a single variable and the whole block could be written or displayed by accessing the same variable. In any event, you can't do it through normal declarations, because the space allocated to the stack is just not this large.

The following program shows how this amount of storage could be allocated to one variable unit:

```
main()
{

        char *a, *malloc();

        if ((a = malloc(60000)) == NULL) {
```

```
            printf("Out of memory");
            exit();
    }

    /* Remainder of program ....... */
```

You now have a pointer that "controls" a large block of memory for whatever purpose you desire.

The memory allocation functions are certainly not limited to char values. Any pointer of any legal data type may contain the address of a **malloc()** assignment. The following program demonstrates this:

```
#include <stdio.h>
main()
{

        int *x, *malloc(), y;

        if ((x = malloc(400)) == NULL) {
                printf("Out of memory\n");
                exit(0);
        }
        else
                for (y = 0; y <= 198; ++x)
                        *(x + y) = 88;

}
```

This program declares an int pointer and also declares **malloc()** in a manner that causes it to return an int pointer. This needs a little explaining. In older C compilers, **malloc()** usually was fixed to return a pointer of type char. However, more recent versions cause **malloc()** to return a void pointer, one that is untyped. This means that it can be conveniently cast into any type of pointer. I question the real effectiveness of this change, as the old char pointer return could also be cast as any type of pointer via the use of the cast operator. However, these new compilers do allow **malloc()** to be declared as any type, so this means that declarations of:

```
char *malloc()
int *malloc()
long *malloc()
etc.
```

automatically cast the function to return the type in the declaration line.

This program uses **malloc()** in a way that causes it to return a pointer of type int, in order to match the data type of the int pointer that will accept the address of the memory block allocated by **malloc().**

In most applications, **malloc()** will be used to return a char pointer, but there are exceptions. This is one of them. The reason for the preference to char pointers lies in the fact that chars utilize 1-byte storage units. Therefore, 400 char units can be stored in a memory block of 400 bytes. However, this program uses an int pointer to access the memory block of 400 characters. Each assignment to `*x` will result in a 2-byte write. Therefore, only 200 int values can be stored in the allocated memory block. If you try to write 400 integer values, thinking that there is memory enough for this purpose, then you will overwrite the 400 bytes of memory that lie at the end of the allocated block. Dangerous!

Note that the **for** loop that loads the block with values of 88 counts from 0 to 198. Each time an int value is written, 2 of the 400 available bytes in the block are used. It must be understood that the argument to **malloc()** is expressed in bytes. However, the construct:

```
*(x + y)
```

deals in storage units. If `y` = 0, then `*x` accesses the first 2 bytes of the block. `*(x + 1)` does not access the second "byte" in the block. It accesses the second storage unit. Since we are dealing with ints, a storage unit is 2 bytes. Therefore, `*(x + 1)` accesses the second storage unit, which falls to the third and fourth bytes in the block. The following minichart may help in picturing this concept:

```
int        *(x + 0)  *(x + 1)  *(x + 2)  *(x + 3)  *(x + 4)

Byte #       0 , 1     2 , 3     4 , 5     6 , 7     8, 9
```

This means that the offset value [i.e., 2 in the expression `*(x + 2)`] can be thought of as half of the block byte position number being accessed. This is not too hard to remember, but different data types (int, long, double, etc.) will also result in different storage units.

While it has not been stated previously, the standard technique of specifying offsets to pointers, as in `*(x + 2)`, may also be expressed in subscripting brackets. For example:

```
*(x + 3) = 88;
```

can also be expressed as:

```
x[3] = 88;
```

One doesn't often see expressions of this type involving declared pointers, the exception often being pointers that have been assigned the address of a block of memory allocated via **malloc()** or some other similar function. In programs that use both arrays and pointers, the bracketed offset designations can become confusing. This is the reason for the availability of the more common `*(x + 2)` offsetting method, which is often used with declared pointers. The two methods offer an expressiveness that tends to keep the two types separate in the mind of the programmer. To add to the possible confusion, offsets within arrays can also be expressed using the unary `*` operator as in:

```
main()
{

        int x[40];
```

```
        *(x + 0) = 65;

        printf("%c\n", *( + 0));

}
```

Near the beginning of this text, it was stated that arrays and pointers could be treated as one and the same in many C operations. These examples just go to show the truthfulness of that statement. However, the conventions that have occurred naturally over the years since the C programming language was authored dictate the use of the unary * operator for memory access via pointers and the bracketed subscripts when dealing with declared arrays.

The following program shows a practical usage of **malloc()** whereby the monochrome screen is read and the contents saved in a memory block. The screen will then be cleared and the contents read back in again. Readers who are using a color-graphics display should change the pointer address to `0xb8000000` in order for this program to work on their systems:

```
#include <stdio.h>
main()
{

        char far *a, *b, *malloc();
        int x;

        a = (char far*) 0xb0000000;

        if ((b = malloc(4000)) == NULL) {
            printf("Out of memory\n");
            exit(0);

        }

        for (x = 0; x < 24; ++x)
             printf("C Language Example of screen storage.\n");

        for (x = 0; x < 4000; ++x)
             *(b + x) = *(a + x);
```

```
        system("cls");
        sleep(5);

        for (x = 0; x < 4000; ++x)
             *(a + x) = *(b + x);

}
```

This program can be compiled using the small-memory-model compiler option and is quite impressive even on the slower 4.77-mHz machines. A `char far` pointer, `a`, is given the address of the screen buffer; a `char` pointer, `b`, is assigned the address of the memory block allocated by **malloc().** Note that **malloc**'s return is tested for `NULL`. The first **for** loop is used to write a sentence to the screen and repeats it so that the entire screen is filled. The next **for** loop reads the contents of the screen a byte at a time. As each byte is read from the screen buffer, it is copied to the memory block through `b`. The copy is made on a byte-for-byte basis. This means that the first byte from the screen [`*(a + 0)`] is copied to the first byte in the block [`*(b + 0)`]. This continues until the 4000th byte from the screen is copied to the 4000th block byte. This completes the copy of the entire screen.

At this point in the execution chain, the monochrome screen is cleared by calling the MS-DOS `"cls"` routine via the C language **system()** function. The **sleep()** function is then called, which will produce a 5-second pause. Without this function, the rewrite to the screen occurs so rapidly after screen clearing that you probably wouldn't be able to see the erasure. The **sleep()** function lets you plainly see that the screen has been cleared.

After 5 seconds, another **for** loop is executed that does the opposite of the former loop. This time, the contents of the memory block are read back into the screen buffer. The copy takes place on a byte-for-byte basis, and all of the original screen information is rewritten in the blink of an eye.

This program could just as easily have transferred the contents to a disk file, but the process would have taken far longer because of the slow operation of mechanical devices. The reading of the disk information back into the cleared screen would take as long. I have written several commercial software packages for C language tutorial purposes that have used routines similar to the one demonstrated by the last program. These programs contained many tutorial screens. Writing the information to these screens in the usual fashion was too slow and would create comprehension difficulties on the part of the student. The solution was to download all screens to disk files. This was done outside of the tutorial program, proper. When I had all the screens on disk, I included these files with the tutorial software. During a program run, several screens were loaded into memory blocks. This was done as soon as the program was executed and was part of the overhead time required for loading all information and before the on-screen run started. Then, when a screen was required, it was loaded directly from a memory block. The write took place almost instantly, and it was possible for the student to switch from one screen to another in a very short time, like flipping the pages of a book.

The following program shows a standard method of saving a screen to a disk and assumes that the screen buffer already contains the information to be saved:

```
#include <stdio.h>
main()
{

        FILE *fp;
        char far *a;
        int x;

        if ((fp = fopen("screen1", "w")) == NULL) {
               printf("Error: Can't open file\n");
               exit(0);
        }

        a = (char far *) 0xb0000000;

        for (x = 0; x < 4000; ++x)
               fputc(*a++, fp);

        fclose(fp);

}
```

This program opens a file in the normal manner, testing for a `NULL` return, which means that the file could not be opened, possibly because of a full disk, a write-protect tab, or some other disk problem. The `char far` pointer, `a`, is given the address of the monochrome-screen buffer. Color-graphics card users will want to change this address assignment to `0xb8000000`, the start of the color-graphics buffer. However, this program assumes that, even when using the color cards, the screen is in the text mode (i.e., screen 0).

Next, a **for** loop is entered, which steps through each of the 4000 byte offsets in the buffer. While only the even-number bytes contain the character information, all bytes are read since the entire screen is to be saved. This means that any special attributes will also be saved. Within the loop, the **fputc()** function is used to write each byte to the disk file. You will notice that the pointer access is stepped by the increment operator *following* the pointer name. This means that the value in `*a` will be returned to the function *before* the pointer is stepped to the next position. Here, we are actually changing the address of the pointer, proper. We could also have written this as:

```
fputc((a + x), fp);
```

which would only add the value of `x` to the address in the pointer, the latter remaining fixed. Either method is acceptable, but the first increments the pointer address while the second uses the pointer address, unchanged, adding the offset to this value. Both result in the same assignments to the disk file.

When the write is complete, the file is closed, and your disk contains a file named `"screen1"`, loaded with all of the screen information.

You could read this information back into the screen by using the slow method shown below:

```
#include <stdio.h>
main()
{
```

```
        FILE *fp;
        char far *a;
        int x;

        if ((fp = fopen("screen1", "r")) == NULL) {
             printf("Error: Cannot open disk\n");
             exit(0);

        a = (char far *) 0xb0000000;

        while ((x = fgetc(fp)) != EOF)
             *a++ = x;

        fclose(fp);

}
```

This is a slow method as seen by the viewer's eye, because a character must be retrieved from the file and then written to the screen. This process is repeated 4000 times until the entire screen has been written.

Note that the **while** loop assigns the return from **fgetc()** to a variable of type int. You might wonder why this line wasn't written as:

```
while ((*a = fgetc(fp)) != EOF)
      *a++;
```

or even:

```
while ((*a++ = fgetc(fp)) != EOF)
      ;
```

Wouldn't the same thing take place, and without having to declare the int variable? The answer is "Yes!"—the same thing would take place—and much more.

The `EOF`, or end-of-file, is defined in **stdio.h** as a value of −1. This means that when the end-of-file condition is reached, **fgetc()**

will return a −1. However, if **fgetc()** is sending its return to a char-type variable, which the char pointer truly is, then there is a big problem. A char is traditionally thought of as an unsigned variable. That is, it can be used to store only positive values and can't handle a minus sign. In modern compilers this is no longer true; a char type can represent both signed and unsigned values. The Turbo C compiler is an example of one that allows for signed values to be stored in char variables. Therefore, the modifications listed above would work. I applaud the great advances made in C language and C compilers with the coming of the still new ANSI standard. However, this signed char business is one feature I don't like. If for no other reason, I feel this way because I believe it contributes to learning difficulties among beginners trying to grasp C language and its rather eerie syntax. I would urge you to continue to think of chars as unsigned, representing positive values only from 0 to 255. If you assume this, even though your compiler may allow for signed values, you will be assured that your programs will maintain portability with other compilers that may not offer this signed feature. If we assume that a char cannot accept a signed number, then `*a` will never return a −1 (`EOF`). This means that the end-of-file is never reached, and the program keeps on looping and writing garbage to memory locations. The screen is filled, and the rest of memory as well!!

Moving on with the program explanation, each value returned to `int x` by **fgetc()** is assigned as the object at the screen buffer location accessed by `a`. While `x` is an int type that stores all values in 2 bytes of memory and `*a` is a char type with only 1 byte of storage, there is no conflict. The value in `x` will be less than 256, and this is a legal value for the `*a` to receive. Since all values of less than 256 are stored solely in the first byte of an int variable (with the second byte being equal to zero), all that occurs is that the second byte value in `x` is simply dropped.

The screen is rewritten, a byte at a time. This will take some time, and the lags will be very obvious to the screen viewer. The following program shows another method of retrieving this code from the disk. The process takes as long for recovery, but the display write is almost instantaneous. The advantages of this will be discussed after program operation is explained:

```
#include <stdio.h>
main()
{

        FILE *fp;
        int x, y;
        char far *a, *b, *malloc();

        a = (char far *) 0xb0000000;

        if ((b = malloc(4000)) == NULL) {
               printf("Out of memory\n");
               exit(0);
        }

        if ((fp = fopen("screen1", "r")) == NULL) {
               printf("Error:Can't open file\n");
               exit(0);
        }

        y = 0;

        while ((x = fgetc(fp)) != EOF)
               *(b + y++) = x;

        fclose(fp);

        printf("Press any key to write screen");
        x = getch();

        for (x = 0; x < 4000; ++x)
               *a++ = *b++;

}
```

This program may seem to be complex to those just learning C, but it can be broken down into small, easy-to-understand modules.

Two `char` pointers are declared, `far a` and (near) `b`. The first is given the address of the monochrome-screen buffer. The second is handed the address of the start of 4000 bytes of memory cleared by **malloc()**. At this point, the file containing the screen information written by a previous program is opened. The **while** loop calls **fgetc(),** which returns the contents of "screen1" in single-byte quantities to variable x. Within the **while** loop, the character value in x is assigned to the byte accessed by pointer b. This byte and all others are within the 4000-byte block set aside by **malloc().** Nothing is written to the screen by this action. Rather, the original screen contents held in this disk file are written to the reserved block of memory containing 4000 bytes. This is a relatively slow process, because each byte must be retrieved from the file and then written into memory. This was the same condition found in the previous program, which wrote the screen directly from the disk file.

Once the memory block has been loaded, a prompt appears telling the user to press any key to write the screen. The **getch()** function is utilized here. It will halt program execution until a character is received. This character serves no purpose in this program other than to release the **getch()** execution halt.

When the key is pressed, a **for** loop is entered and the contents from the memory block are written directly to the screen. Pointer b returns the byte from the memory block, which is written to the screen through access by far pointer a. This method was demonstrated in an earlier program.

This program does not get the contents to the screen any quicker than did the previous program, but the time between actually starting and ending the write is tremendously fast. The time overhead comes from the necessity of loading the information from a disk file.

The thing to do when several pages of information are desired is to load them all in at the same time. Once the screens have been copied to memory blocks, they can be accessed almost instantaneously. From the user's point of view, it is far more pleasing to get the long loading process over with during the initial call-up or execution of the program. Of course, multiple pages will require more memory block allocations. The number of pages that can be loaded into memory will depend on the amount of memory your machine has and also on the memory-model compiler version. Large-memory models are able to allocate more memory than small-memory models can.

There are functions available in Turbo C and most other C compilers that will allow for block transfers of memory. In Turbo C, functions such as **movemem()** or **movedata()** will allow you to forego the looping routines that read or write data from or to memory locations. This will drastically decrease the complexity of your source code.

Calloc()

Most of the attention to memory allocation functions has surrounded the use of **malloc().** As you will recall, **malloc()** simply finds a free block in memory and then returns a pointer to it. **Calloc()** works in a similar fashion, except that it is more convenient when storage must be allocated for storage units of more than 1 byte. Also, **calloc()** clears all memory blocks as a part of its operation. This means that a block of 4000 bytes allocated by **calloc()** will return a pointer to a block whose bytes have been set to 0 (zero). The following program is similar to another example in this chapter but effectively demonstrates one of the advantages **calloc()** offers:

```
#include <stdio.h>
main()
{

        int *x, y, *calloc();

        if ((x = calloc(400, 2)) == NULL) {
             printf("Out of memory\n");
             exit(0);
        }

        for (y = 0; y < 400; ++y)
              *(x + y) = 88;

}
```

Referring to the earlier program that assigned the address of a 400-byte memory block to an int pointer, you will remember that int values numbering a maximum of 200 were all that could be written to the block. An int value requires 2 bytes of storage. In this example, another int pointer is used. **Calloc()** is called in a format of:

```
calloc(storage_units, unit_size)
```

The arguments express number of storage units and unit size. Therefore, the usage of **calloc()** in this program does not mean that a block of 400 bytes is allocated. Rather, the block is 800 bytes long. The number of storage units is 400, but the size of each storage unit is 2 bytes. Therefore, (400 * 2) = 800 bytes. This program can safely address from 0 to 399 units in this block without overwriting memory. This means that `*(x + 399)` will access the 799th and 400th bytes in the allocated block. But we don't have to worry about this aspect of storage after an allocation for the desired number of storage units has been made. **Malloc()** requires arguments in the form of bytes. Arguments to **calloc()** deal with storage units.

Throughout this text, I have been careful to point out that stated storage sizes for various data types apply only to "most MS-DOS machines." This is important, because C language offers excellent portability and is often used on minicomputers and very large systems. On these other types of machines, a standard int type may be allocated 4 bytes of storage; a long, 8 bytes; and so on. Storage allocations for all data types in C are relative and are based on the architecture of the machine and many other factors.

The built-in argument protocol of **calloc()** allows for portability to many other types of machines . . . if the arguments are stated correctly. In the previous program, **calloc()** was used in the form of:

```
calloc(400, 2)
```

The desire here was to set aside 400 storage units for int values, an int requiring 2 bytes of storage. This is all well and good when dealing with an MS-DOS machine, but suppose that the program containing this use of **calloc()** is to be ported to many other types of computers. There is no portability, because other machines may have other sizes (other than 2 bytes) for int values. The way to maintain portability is to test the size of storage on the machine that will run the software. That is, base **calloc**'s allocation on the storage size, which is tested while the program is running. How is that done?

Simple! All full-function C compilers contain the **sizeof()** function, which has been used sparingly in some of the program examples in this text. This function returns the size in bytes of any variable and, unknown to more than a few C programmers, the size of any data type specified. That is:

```
sizeof(int)
```

will return the size of an int data type. Here, `int` is a keyword that can be read directly by the function. Now, if this function were executed on an MS-DOS machine, **sizeof()** would return a value of 2, but on a mainframe, it might return 4 or more bytes.

With this in mind, **calloc()** could have been used in the previous program in this manner:

```
calloc(400, sizeof(int));
```

This usage would assure that the correct number of bytes were set aside for the storage of 400 int data types, regardless of the amount of storage allocated to int data types. The **calloc()** function is already portable. You should make certain that your arguments to it and other such functions are equally portable.

There is nothing magic about the way **calloc()** performs its task. In fact, it simply calls **malloc()**. The following is an example of how **malloc()** can be used to provide the portability of **calloc()**:

```
malloc(400 * sizeof(int))
```

Here, the argument to **malloc()** is a mathematical expression. The number of bytes is expressed as storage units multiplied by the size of the individual unit. This is exactly what **calloc()** does within its source code structure. The only difference between these two functions is that when **malloc()** is used in this manner, it does not reset all allocated bytes to NULL or zero.

As a side note, once an allocated block of memory has been used for a particular purpose, it should be freed for possible allocation to later program portions. This assumes that the program will continue to run long after the allocated block is no longer needed. To free a block of memory that was allocated with either **malloc()** or **calloc()**, use the **free()** function in the form of:

```
free(ptr)
```

where `ptr` is the pointer to the block of allocated memory.

Summary

When a pointer is assigned the memory address of an allocated block of memory, then we can say that the pointer has been initialized and, in a manner of speaking, has been "sized" to the number of bytes in the storage area. It is then safe to copy objects to this memory block using the pointer for access. In other words, the pointer may be treated as an array of the same size as the memory block the pointer addresses.

Both of the standard C language memory allocation functions will return a NULL character if the amount of memory requested cannot be allocated. Any program that uses either of these functions must test their returns for the NULL. If you assume that the storage space is available and it turns out that it isn't, then any writes attempted will become memory overwrites with the inherent dangers that these occurrences present.

In the Turbo C compiler and most other modern-day equivalents, **malloc()** and **calloc()** return pointers of type void. This means that the return address value can assume any legal pointer data type. This casting can be done in the declaration line, declaring ***malloc()** or ***calloc()** to be char, int, long, double, or whatever. If either of these functions is to be used for multiple allocations to several different types of pointers, then the cast operator can be used in each case. Older C compilers usually configured **malloc()** and **calloc()** to return a pointer of type char.

Through the use of C language pointers and the memory allocation functions, it is convenient to do block reads and block writes. These were demonstrated in this chapter by programs that read, wrote, and rewrote the monochrome-graphics screen. Such operations are certainly not limited to the visual display screens and may be used to read and write any block of memory anywhere in the system. The reason for the screen buffer examples lies in the fact that the memory writes can actually be seen. This is far more expressive, far more "visual" from a tutorial standpoint.

Chapter 8

Pointers and Functions

While pointers are useful, powerful, and indispensable throughout all phases of C language programming, their capabilities yield high-powered program performance especially when dealing with programmed functions.

We already know that arguments are passed to and from functions by value. It is not possible to change the value of a calling program variable within a function . . . unless we have the address of a variable in the calling program.

C language functions can return values that can be, in turn, assigned to variables within the calling program, but through pointer operations, we can write specialized functions that will return a value to the calling program and change the values in other variables whose memory addresses are handed to the function. In this manner, it is possible to write a function that, figuratively, "returns" many values in a single operation.

Again, the direct programming of pointers is what gives C language its power, expressiveness, and authority. It is also the pointer that has vaulted C language to the top of the list of languages most desirable for software development.

The following program incorporates a special function to return the square of a value passed to it. This is a useless function for any but tutorial purposes, but as the discussion continues other examples will be provided that will provide some practical application tools. The program follows:

```
main()
{

        int x, y;

        x = 12;
        y = 7;

        x = square(x);
        y = square(y);

        printf("%d  %d\n", x, y);

}
int square(a)
int a;
{

        return(a * a);

}
```

The **square()** function is passed a value from the calling program. This value is assigned to `a`, a variable that is internal to the function. The function return value is `a * a`, or the square of the passed value. This program will display the values:

```
144  49
```

on the monitor screen. In the calling program, **square()** is called twice, because it was necessary to obtain the square of two different values. It is not possible for a function in C to directly return two values. In this example, the function "equates" to the square of its passed value.

This next example shows how a similar function can accept the value of a calling variable *and* the memory address of another. The passed value is returned by the function, just as in the above example. However, the address is used to reassign another variable to its square. The result is a function that returns a square value in the normal manner and rewrites one via a pointer. The program follows:

```
main()
{

        int x, y;

        x = 12;
        y = 7;

        x = square(x, &y);

        printf("%d  %d\n", x, y);

}
int square(a, b)
int a, *b;
{

        *b = *b * *b;
        return(a * a);

}
```

This program will also display 144 and 49 on the screen, but the function was called only once, which results in a faster program run. In the function, a is a standard int-type variable, but b is a pointer of type int. Notice that the memory address of y in the calling program was passed to the function. This address was assigned to pointer b in the function. The expression:

```
*b = *b * *b;
```

will look a bit weird at first glance because of the number of asterisks. The first two are the unary * operator accessing the object at the address passed to the pointer. The third asterisk is the multiplicative operator, while the third is another unary * operator. If b were a standard variable, then this line would read:

```
b = b * b;
```

The multiple use of symbols to perform different operations in C is a very good reason to stick to the source code formatting conventions that were established many years ago. This means that all arithmetic operators should be separated from their variable names by a space as in:

```
x = a * b;
```

rather than:

```
x=a*b;
```

The former provides much better clarity of understanding. The multiplication of pointer b could also be written in C shorthand as:

```
*b *= *b;
```

which means the same thing as:

```
*b = *b * *b;
```

Either way, there are still a lot of asterisks. But suppose that these examples did not adhere to the source code formatting conventions. We might end up with a combination of:

```
*b=*b**b;
```

which is not easier to understand than the shorthand method, bastardized by poor program formatting:

```
*b*=*b;
```

If you have not been adhering to the formatting standards displayed in the original K&R "The C Programming Language," then perhaps you might wish to familiarize yourself with these "rules of good etiquette" for the C programmer. I have observed that, as C becomes more popular and the subject of more and more books, there is a breakdown in these formatting conventions. Even the Turbo C reference works and those of other popular C compiler suppliers are getting "sloppy" in this regard. This is not elitism on my part. Rather, it is an appeal. The writing of sloppy-looking source code, regardless of the fact that it compiles and runs properly, can quickly become a detriment to newcomers learning this language. Also, it's getting harder for those of use who are supposed to know something about C to figure out some of the "garbled" programs we see displayed hither and yon. More on this later!

The example of a function returning a value, supposedly for assignment to another variable in the calling program, and changing the value of another calling program variable is not especially unique, although it does not follow a typical function programming pattern. More than likely, the operation would be handled by sending two address values to the function and returning nothing or void. The following program demonstrates this:

```
main()
{

        int x, y;

        x = 12;
        y = 7;

        square(&x, &y);

        printf("%d  %d\n", x, y);

}
```

```
void square(a, b)
int *a, *b;
{

        *a *= *a;
        *b *= *b;

}
```

The same result is had within the calling program, and the function source code is a little more "typical" of what one might expect.

In all of these examples, the function expected a specific number of arguments, and had to be passed this same number to prevent an error. But what about functions that accept a varying number of arguments? A good example of this is **printf()**, which can be used in, seemingly, different formats, including:

```
printf("hello, world\n");
printf("%s\n", "hello, world");
printf("%d\n", x);
printf("%d %c\n", x, y);
```

How is this apparent bevy of arguments handled? The following discussion will answer part of this question:

```
main()
{

        int x, y;

        x = 17;
        y = 134;

        newprintf("%d %d", x, y);

}
```

```
void newprint(str, args)
char *str;
int args;
{

        printf("%s\n%d", str, args);

}
```

This program declares and assigns two int variables and then calls a new function, arbitrarily named **newprint()**. The arguments to **newprint()** are handled just like they would be if **printf()** were being used. The **newprint()** function source code at the bottom of the calling program declares only two arguments in its parentheses, `str` and `args`. The first is declared a char pointer, the second is an int. This is a test program/function purely for discussion purposes, so the first job at hand is to see what the two arguments yield. We'll use the standard **printf()** function to display the values of the two arguments. The screen will display:

```
%d  %d
17
```

This means that `str` points to the string that was enclosed in quotation marks within the original call to **newprint()**. We learned much earlier that a quoted constant in C actually returns the address of that constant in memory. Therefore, `str` points to the string constant "`%d  %d`". We can say, loosely, that `str` is that quoted string from the calling program. Variable `args` is displayed as 17, the value of the first variable argument to **newprint()**. However, you will recall that two variable arguments were provided. Only one is displayed. The reason for this is that our **print()** function within **newprint()** called for only one int argument in its format control string. However, `args` is only a single argument, so what do we do?

Here is where pointers come into play. Although this program doesn't show it, `args` contains both variable arguments originally made to **newprint()**. For now, we will say that `args` represents a block of memory that contains all of the values handed to

newprint() during the initial call. The first 2 bytes contain the value of x (17) from the calling program. The second 2 bytes contain the value in y or 134. These values are aligned sequentially at the start of storage reserved for args. Incidentally, this storage was set aside automatically by the calling program when the **newprint()** function was invoked. Without going into unnecessary detail, let's just say this is the manner in which C handles function calls.

The following program reveals more about this discussion:

```
main()
{

     int x, y;

     x = 17;

     y = 134;

     newprint("%d  %d", x, y);

}
newprint(str, args)
char *str;
int args;
{

     int *ptr;

     ptr = &args;

     printf("%s\n%d\n%d\n", str, *ptr, *(ptr + 1));

}
```

This program will display:

```
%d  %d
17
134
```

This is what we are looking for. The big change in the function source code lies in the use of `ptr`, a pointer of type `int` that has been declared within the function. It was stated earlier that `args` contained all of the second argument group passed to **newprint()**. The first argument group is the formatting string enclosed in quotes. Therefore, the storage address of `args` is the place to begin. Pointer `ptr` is given the address of `args` via the unary `&` operator. Now, `*ptr` contains the object value of the first argument to **newprint()** (after the format string), and `*(ptr + 1)` contains the second.

Let's shuffle the deck a bit by changing the calling arguments slightly in the following program:

```
main()
{

    int x, y;
    char a[20];

    x = 17;
        y = 134;

    strcpy(a, "Today");

    newprint("%d  %d  %s", x, y, a);

}
newprint(str, args)
char *str;
int args;
{

    int *ptr;

    ptr = &args;

    printf("%s\n%d\n%d\n%s", str, *ptr, *(ptr + 1), *(ptr + 2));

}
```

This program will display:

```
%d  %d  %s
17
134
Today
```

Again, `*ptr` returns the 2 bytes that make up 17; `*(ptr + 1)` gives us 134, and `*(ptr + 3)` returns the address of the storage location of "`Today`". What it amounts to is the storage location starting at variable `args` forms a memory "chain" of actual values and/or addresses of strings.

Of course, we are cheating a lot, since the supposed purpose of **newprint()** is to replace the **printf()** function common to all versions of C. Since **newprint()** calls **printf(),** this new function doesn't really take its place. The purpose of this discussion is to illustrate argument alignment in function calls, but to avoid being accused of "copping out," I will explain the workings of **printf()** a little more.

The format string in **printf()** is the controlling element for reading the second argument grouping content. First of all, it must be remembered that if we want to print the letter `'C'` to the screen, this letter does not reside, as a letter or character, anywhere in memory. It is stored, as is all data, as a numeric value. The ASCII value of `'C'` is 67 decimal.

The **printf()** source code is long and complex, because the function has to read the contents of the format control string and build up a character string accordingly. If the first element in the control string is a `%d`, the **printf()** source code instructs the function to access `*ptr` (using the above example as a reference) or `*(ptr + 0)`, if you prefer, and retrieve an `int` value. If the content of the first 2 bytes addressed by the pointer is 17 and 0, this means that the numeric value equal to 17 is to be displayed as a decimal integer. However, we are writing to the screen, so we can't simply poke a 17 in at a character location. No, **printf()** has to place the character `'1'` followed by the character `'7'` in the display string it is building internally. The single number 17 is represented as two characters, a `'1'` and a `'7'`. The `'1'` is represented by ASCII 49 and the `'7'` by ASCII 55. Therefore, the values that must be poked to the display screen buffer to represent numeric 17 are

49 and 55. This is a long conversion from 17 and 0, the 2-byte storage for the number, 17. This process applies to all other numeric values as well, with the larger numbers requiring a larger number of characters to represent them.

After the first two characters representing numeric 17 are placed at the front of the display string being built by the function, the format control string is read again, starting at a point just following the `%d`. Assume that the next read yields a space. This signals no special code, so it is displayed as the whitespace character that is printed when the keyboard space bar is pressed. The space character has a value of ASCII 32, so this value is added to the screen display string, which now reads:

```
49 55 32
```

The next format string read yields another `%d`. This signals **printf()** to go to the next pointer position, `*(ptr + 1)`, and retrieve 2 bytes of integer data. The value returned goes through the same process as for the value of 17, discussed earlier. We'll assume that the retrieved integer value is 28, which yields an ASCII character string of 50 56. The screen string building in **printf()** now reads:

```
49 55 32 50 56
```

Again **printf()** goes back to the remainder of its format string. Let's assume that it next discovers another whitespace character. This character signals no special code, as does `%d`, for example, so the character is to be displayed as a space on the screen. The ASCII code for a space is 32. The character string for the screen will read:

```
49 55 32 50 56 32
```

Once again, the format string is read, and this time a `%s` pops up. This signals a string value and **printf()** goes to the next argument vector of `*(x + 2)`. Here it looks for an address of a string, a pointer. It accesses that address location from the 2 bytes used by the pointer for storage (the assumption here is that a small-memory-model compiler defaulting to 2-byte pointers is used) and copies the numeric byte contents to the end of the screen string it is building. If we assume that the string content is "ABC" then 65, 66, and 67 are copied to the internal screen display string, which now reads:

```
49 55 32 50 56 32 65 66 67
```

This is the end of the format control string, so **printf()** is now ready to dump these contents. The following program should be familiar as it pokes bytes to the monochrome screen:

```
main()
{

        char far *a, s[10];
        int x, y;

        a = (char far *) 0xb0000000;

        s[0] = 49;
        s[1] = 55;
        s[2] = 32;
        s[3] = 50;
        s[4] = 56;
        s[5] = 32;
        s[6] = 65;
        s[7] = 66;
        s[8] = 67;

        y = 0;
        for (x = 0; x < 18; x += 2)
             *(a + x) = s[y++];

}
```

This program will display:

```
17 28 ABC
```

on the screen.

This has been a laborious process and doesn't even begin to reveal all of the complex workings of **printf()**. Please understand that this explanation has been a very brief and technically symbolic representation of the "processes" that a function like **printf()** must go through in order to deliver the screen output that we take for granted. This discussion has also revealed how a function can be written to handle an indeterminate amount of passed argument values. Without pointers, such operations would not be available to the programmer.

The concepts explained lead to other possibilities, such as functions that will perform mathematical operations on any number of arguments. The **add()** function is demonstrated by the following program:

```
main()
{

        int a, b, c, d, e, f;

        a = 12;
        b = 4;
        c = 8;
        d = 234;

        e = add(4, a, b, c, d);
        f = add(3, b, c, d);

        printf("%d\n", e);
        printf("%d\n", f);

}
int add(args)
int args;
{

        int tot, x, y, *ptr;

        ptr = &args;
```

```
        y = *ptr++;
        tot = 0;

        for (x = 0; x < y; ++x)
              tot += *ptr++;

        return(tot);

}
```

This program assigns values to four `int` variables and then calls `add()` two times, which returns the total of all its arguments to variables `e` and `f`. This program displays:

```
258
246
```

on the screen.

The **add()** function accepts any number of integer arguments, but the first argument *must* state the number of arguments passed. The first call to **add()** uses four values to be added, so the first argument is 4. The second call uses a first argument of 3 in order to add the three values in the variable arguments that follow.

There is no format string in this function. None is needed, as the first argument is all that is necessary to effect the add operation. The only argument shown as being passed to **add()** is named `args` and resides within the body of the function. As before, `args` is the start of memory where all arguments to **add()** have been placed. The declared pointer is given the address of `args` and the first value is extracted. The expression:

```
y = *ptr++;
```

does two things. First, the object value at the address contained within the pointer is returned to `y`. Then, the pointer address is incremented by one *storage unit,* in this case, 2 bytes. The value in `y` is the first argument to **add().** On the first call to this function, `y` is equal to 4. Variable `y`, then, contains the total number of arguments to be added by the function. Another internal variable, tot, is assigned an initial value of zero. This will be the variable that will contain the added totals.

Next, a **for** loop is entered, which increments x from a value of 0 (zero) to a value that is one less than y. Remember, y contains the number of arguments to be added. Counting from 0 to 1 less than y will cause the loop to cycle the number of times in y. Remember, the loop count begins at zero . . . not one. Assuming four arguments to be added, looping from 0 to 3 (y − 1) will yield four loop cycles.

Pointer, *ptr,* has already been incremented to the next data position before the loop is entered. This incrementing was handled during the object assignment to y. On the first pass of the loop, *(ptr + 1) is accessed for a return value of 12 (the value of the passed argument in a). The pointer is actually advanced by the increment operator, but *(ptr + 1) is another way of expressing its relative position. This value is added to the current value of tot, which is zero at this stage. On the next pass, *(ptr + 2) is accessed and added to the current value of tot. This variable is now equal to 16 (12 + 4). On the next pass, the 8 is added and on the next, 234 is added to the total in tot. The loop times out, because it has cycled four times. The value in tot is now equal to the sum of the four arguments. This value is returned to the calling program, where it is assigned to e.

The next call to **add()** contains only three values to be added, so the first argument is 3. The same operations begin all over, except that the loop will cycle only three times because of the new value in y. This time, the total of the three arguments to **add()** will be returned.

Pointers to Functions

A C language function is not a variable, but you can declare pointers to functions that can be used in a manner that other pointers are used, such as placing them in arrays, or passed to other functions. One doesn't see a lot of use of pointers to functions, but this technique can sometimes be used to advantage. One common usage of pointers to a function is in purposely hiding the intent of a program. Pointers to functions serve to hide the name and source code of that function. Muddying the waters is not a normal routine in C programming, but with the security placed on software these days, there is an element of misdirection that seems to be growing.

The following program demonstrates the basic technique of declaring a pointer to a function:

```
main()
{

        int strlen(), x;
        char a[15];

        strcpy(a, "COMPUTER");

        x = scarp(a, strlen);

        printf("%d\n", x);

}
int scarp(c, girl)
char *c;
int (*girl) ();
{

        return((*girl) (c));
}
```

This process may look a little ridiculous, and maybe it is, but it does effectively demonstrate a pointer to a function. In this case, the function in question is **strlen()**, which returns the length of a string argument. Notice that **strlen()** is declared as a part of the calling program. This is a necessity, even though the function is a part of the linked library code.

Within the calling program, another function is invoked. **Scarp()**, arbitrarily named, passes two values. The first is the char array, which now contains "COMPUTER". The second is the name of the **strlen()** function, proper. In this usage, `strlen` without parentheses is the address of the **strlen()** function.

Within **scarp()**, the address of `a` is given to `char *c`, and the address of `strlen` is passed on to a pointer to this function arbitrarily named `girl`. Note the declaration of this entity within the function. The expression:

```
int (*girl) ()
```

says that `girl` is a pointer to a function that returns an int value.

At this juncture, the expression (`*girl`) may be used exactly as you would **strlen()**. In the function:

```
return((*girl) (c));
```

means exactly the same thing as:

```
return(strlen(c));
```

`*(girl) ()` points to the storage address set aside for **strlen()** when it is declared in the program.

Passing Two-Dimensional Arrays to Functions

When passing an entire two-dimensional array as an argument to a function, we lose a bit of versatility that might otherwise be had. The following program fragment is an example:

```
main()
{

        char a[4][9];

        strcpy(a[0], "hello");

        strcpy(a[1], "goodbye");
        strcpy(a[2], "zebra");
        strcpy(a[3], "horse");
```

```
        pt(a, 4);

}
void pt(c, i)
int i;
char c[4][9];
{

        int x;

        for (x = 0; x < i; ++x)
                printf("%s\n", c[x]);

}
```

The program under discussion declares a two-dimensional `char` array and loads it with four strings. In C, there is no array bounds checking, so a second argument (`i`) is passed to the function (along with the pointer to the array), specifying the number of strings. Within the function, the contents of the two-dimensional array argument are displayed on the screen. As has often been the case, this function is useless for anything but a tutorial discussion. However, it does show access to a passed two-dimensional array. The concept here can be applied to any other function that must access an array of this type, say, for sorting purposes or any other purpose imaginable.

However, we are somewhat inconvenienced by the protocol that *must* be used when passing arrays of strings to a function. The function must be told the parameters of the array. Since array `a` in the calling program was declared with four lines and nine columns, the same is specified within the function. Actually, the lines designation is unimportant, but columns must be specified. With this in mind, the function could have been written as:

```
void pt(c, i)
int i;
char c[][9];
{

            etc...........
```

If we assume that **pt()** is designed to be called by any program, then there is a problem of accommodating different array sizes. The only answer is to size the array in the function so that it can handle any pointer to a two-dimensional array that might be passed to it. We might write **pt()** in the following manner:

```
pt(c, i)
int i;
char c[][300];
{

        etc..........
```

This means that the largest number of lines in the array is virtually unlimited, and the maximum length of any string is 300 characters, including the NULL. This would probably be adequate for most purposes, and the array within the function can be made even larger if necessary. However, this overly large array consumes data storage space and is simply not efficient. If the array argument passed to this function contained only 10 strings, each with a maximum of 10 characters, the array within the function would be 30 times oversized for this purpose.

There are several ways around this problem. The most obvious way is to declare an array of pointers as is shown in the following program:

```
main()
{

        char *a[4];

        a[0] = "hello";
        a[1] = "goodbye";
        a[2] = "zebra";
        a[3] = "horse";

        pt(a, 4);

}
```

```
void pt(c, i);
int i;
char *c[];
{

        int x;

        for (x = 0; x < i; ++x)
             printf("%s\n", c[x]);

}
```

This is more convenient in one way and also saves on storage, since `char *c` in the function is made the same size as the passed array of pointers. Note that it is still necessary to pass the number of string pointers in the array as a separate argument.

This routine will work fine as long as constants are to be used as the array strings. However, many array operations load data from disk files, from the keyboard, and from many other sources where a *copy* of data to allocated memory is necessary. From past lessons, we know that you can't (or shouldn't) copy any data to a pointer. This leaves us with a couple of alternatives. First of all, each element in the array of pointers could be allocated storage space using **malloc()**. The following program shows how this technique might be used to store keyboard input data:

```
#include <stdio.h>
main()
{

     char *a[4]; b[256], *malloc();
     int x;

     for (x = 0; x < 4; ++x) {
          gets(b);
          if ((a[x] = *malloc(strlen(b) + 1)) == NULL) {
               printf("Out of memory\n");
               exit(0);

          }
```

```
                else
                        strcpy(a[x], b);


        }


        pt(a, 4);

}
pt(c, i)
int i;
char *c[];
{

        int x;

        for (x = 0; x < i; ++x)
                printf("%s\n", c[x]);

}
```

This method will cover all storage situations, but there is a higher programming overhead in regard to the amount of extra code that must be input. Actually, the char array method has its advantages in this type of operation, but you always have to declare, within the function, the array bounds. There is a way around this, however, and it doesn't require a lot of extra source code. The following program demonstrates this new concept:

```
main()
{

        char a[4][9];

        strcpy(a[0], "hello");
        strcpy(a[1], "goodbye");
        strcpy(a[2], "zebra");
        strcpy(a[3], "horse");

        pt(a, 4, 9);

}
```

```
pt(c, i, len)
int i, len;
char *c;
{

    int x;
    for (x = 0; x < i; ++x) {
        printf("%s\n", c);
        c += len;

}
```

This solves the problem completely. Instead of declaring a two-dimensional `char` array within the function, a `char` pointer is declared. It contains the address of the start of the two-dimensional array in the calling program or `&a[0]`. The **pt()** function argument chain has been changed by adding a third argument. This value states the number of storage units the original array contains. Since the array column value is 9, this is the value passed on to the function and is represented by the variable `len`. Within the function, the **for** loop steps `x` from a value of zero to 1 less than `i`. The latter variable contains the number of lines in the initial array. This means that all four strings will be accessed (*Note:* 0 to 3 makes up four elements.) Within the **for** loop, the pointer address is incremented by the value in `len`.

This procedure allows the function to be conveniently used with any array argument, but the overhead lies in having to pass one more argument to the function. There is a higher storage overhead as well, when compared to the previous program example using an array of pointers. The reason for this is that each pointer in the array of pointers was allocated storage based on a measured string length. In this last program example, the array from the calling program was allocated the number of columns specified (nine). If a string is less than nine characters in length, then extra storage is wasted. However, since the array from the calling program will be sized according to the programmer's needs, this should not be a costly waste of memory.

The size of the array from the calling program makes no different whatsoever to the function, as long as the proper arguments are supplied. In effect, arguments `i` and `len` within the function would seem to exactly reflect the subscript values. They do in this example and the value in `len` must always be equal to the column value of the array argument. However, the lines value (`i`) need not encompass the entire storage "capability" of the array but only the number of strings to be accessed. In the above example, array `a` was sized to store four string arguments, each with a maximum length of nine characters including NULL. Additionally, four strings were copied to the array. However, if the call to **pt()** had been:

```
pt(a, 2, 9);
```

then only the first two strings would have been displayed. Therefore, we can say that `i` expresses the number of strings to be accessed in any array argument, and `len` always expresses the number of column positions (maximum allocated storage for one string) in the array argument.

Functions Returning Pointers

For some reason, there is a kind of fear among the ranks of beginning C programmers about pointers in general. Hopefully, the discussions that have already been presented have lessened these concerns. However, the subject of functions that return pointers seems to be even more frightening. There is no reason for such a fear.

Previously, it has been shown how pointer arguments to functions can be used to alter a value in the calling program. In these cases, no pointer values were returned from the function. The address value passed to the function was used for accessing a variable's address to make changes in memory.

The following program calls a function that returns a pointer of type `char`:

```
main()
{

        char a[10], b[10], *p, *combine();

        strcpy(a, "horse");
        strcpy(b, "fly");

        p = combine(a, b);

        printf("%s\n", p);

}
char *combine(s, t)
char *s, *t;
{

        int x, y;
        char r[100];

        strcpy(r, s);
        y = strlen(r);
        for (x = y; *t != '\0'; ++x)
                r[x] = *t++;

        r[x] = '\0';

        return(r);

}
```

This program will display:

```
        horsefly
```

on the monitor screen. The **combine()** function is nothing more than a version of **strcat()** that returns a pointer to the combined string and doesn't alter the value of any of its argument objects.

The program declares two `char` arrays, a `char` pointer, *and* it declares `*combine()` to be a function that returns a `char` pointer value. This declaration must be made in order to let **main()** know what type of return is expected. Two string constants, "horse" and "fly," are copied to the two arrays. Next, **combine()** is called in the format of:

```
p = combine(a, b);
```

Now, `p` is a pointer of type `char`. Therefore, it must be handed the address of a `char`-type object. This means the return from **combine()** must be a `char` pointer.

Skipping to the function source code, we see that the function is declared for a `char *` return by the opening line:

```
char *combine(s, t);
```

This means that, on return, the function will equate to a `char` pointer. Variables `s` and `t` are declared `char` pointers by the next line in the function.

Within the function body, `x` and `y` are declared `ints`, and `r` is declared a `char` array with 100 bytes for storage. The subscript value need only be adequate to store the strings of `s` and `t` combined.

The **strcpy()** function is called to copy the string pointed to by `s` into `r[]`. Next, **strlen()** returns the number of characters in `r[]` and assigns this returned int value to `y`. A **for** loop is entered, which assigns `x` a starting value of `y`. Since `y` is equal to the number of bytes in `r`, and `r` presently holds the contents of the string pointed to by `s`, this means that `x` will start its count at a value that is equal to the position of the NULL byte in `r[]`, since `x` is assigned an initial loop value of `y`, the latter being equal to 5. Let me say this in another way. The string pointed to by argument `s` has been copied into the `r` array. The end of this string is terminated by a NULL. **Strlen()** returns the number of characters in `r[]`. We know that `s` points to "`horse`," a string containing five characters. When "`horse`" is copied into `r[]`, **strlen(r)** returns a value of 5. The character in `r[]` at the fifth offset (`r[5]`) is the NULL.

When the loop starts cycling, the initial value of `x` is 5. On the first pass, the NULL byte in `r[]` is overwritten by the first byte pointed to by t, as in:

```
r[x] = *t++;
```

Pointer t is incremented by one, and the loop cycles again. On the next pass, x = 6, so the byte i[6] receives the next character in *t.

On each pass of the loop, the exit clause is tested. In this loop, the exit clause is:

```
*t != '\0'
```

Many programmers think that the second expression in a **for** loop must set the maximum value (or minimum value in negative-going loops) for the loop variable, in this case x. This is not true! This portion of the loop statement is an exit clause and may contain any legal expression. In this example, the loop will terminate when *t is equal to NULL or '\0'. Each time r[x] = *t++ is executed within the loop, pointer t is incremented. Before another loop cycle, the expression *t != '0\' is evaluated. When the end of the string in t is reached, the loop will be exited.

Since we know that t points to "fly," we also know that the loop will cycle three times. After the third pass, the exit clause brings about a loop exit. However, the loop variable has already been incremented in readiness for the next pass. Even though this pass never came about, x is set the the next logical byte in r[]. Since the termination of the loop occurred when the NULL character in t was encountered, this NULL was never written to the end of r[]. Therefore, the contents of r[] encompass a series of discrete characters and *not* a string. A NULL terminator is required to make a string. So, the contents of r[] are made into an "official" C string by:

```
r[x] = '\0';
```

This puts the finishing touch on the whole operation; r[] now stores a bona fide string.

The rest is simple. All we have to do is pass a pointer to r back to the calling program. The expression:

```
return(r);
```

is the obvious and correct choice. Remember, `r`, used without subscripting brackets, is a pointer to the contents of this array. This address value is passed back to the calling program and assigned to pointer `p`. When `p` is handed to the **printf()** function, the display of "`horsefly`" is the end result.

The complexities with this function lie in manually concatenating "`fly`" to "`horse`." The return of a pointer by the function is child's play. The following is a commented listing of the above function that may add a bit more clarity to its operation:

```
char *combine(s, t)   /* Return a char pointer to caller */
char *s, *t;          /* s and t are char pointers */
{

     int x, y;              /* x and y are ints */
     char r[100];           /* r is a char array with 100 bytes */

     strcpy(r, s);          /* copy string pointed to by s into r */
     y = strlen(r);         /*get the length of the string to y */

     for (x = y; *t != '\0'; ++x) /* count x starting at x = y */
          r[x] = *t++;      /* read byte from t into r */

     r[x] = '\0';      /* tack on NULL */

     return(r);     /* return a pointer to the internal array */

}
```

Again, this program calls a function that *returns* a char pointer, it does not alter the object values of either of its two pointer arguments.

Summary

C language functions are like completely separate programs. When called by a program, the function takes control. This control is not returned to the calling program until the function returns a value (via the return statement) or until the function execution chain is completed.

Arguments are passed to pointers *by value.* This means that when `x` is an argument to a function, it is the value that `x` represents and not the variable and its assigned storage area that is passed. A like variable is created within the function to store the *value* of `x` that was passed.

We do not have access (within the function) to the variables themselves when they are used as arguments to functions. However, the address of a variable or other object in memory may be passed to a function, again by value. When the function knows the address of an object in memory, then it can directly address that object and make changes or retrieve information. If the value of an object is to be changed by a function, then the address of the object must be passed, and not the value of the object.

When multiple arguments are passed to a function, an argument list is contained in memory. Within the function, a pointer to the first argument can be used to access all of the list, provided that there is a specific indication of what kind of and how many arguments were passed to the function. The inner workings of the **printf()** function access arguments in this manner, with the format string indicating the exact nature of the arguments that follow.

Pointers to functions are possible and, sometimes, practical. While a function is not a variable, it is possible to define pointers to functions that can be passed to other functions, placed in arrays, and used to manipulate data.

Functions are often used to read and write data in the calling program by being passed the memory address of an object. Likewise, it is quite simple to write a function that actually returns a memory address or pointer. To do this, the function itself must be declared in the calling program as a function that returns a pointer as in:

```
char *combine();
```

Additionally, the source code of the function must contain a heading of the return type such as:

```
char *combine()
```

These declarations inform the calling environment as to the return "intentions" of the function.

The ability to easily incorporate new functions is a strong aspect of the C programming language. Since these functions are actually separate programs that have no relationship with the calling program, other than through the arguments that are specifically passed back and forth, pointers provide a direct means of communication. By passing memory addresses, the function is provided a pathway into certain areas of the calling program, and can make changes and exchange information. Pointers are often the power behind C language function operations.

Chapter 9

Pointers to Other Objects

The pointer types discussed so far in this text have all been of standard data types and usually were directed to point to the address of a declared variable or to a known memory location to be read or written.

Of course, pointers can also be given the address of a function, and point to it. If you think about it long enough, you will soon realize that anything within a program lies in memory; therefore, a pointer can point to any part of the program.

This chapter will explore some of the other "entities" that pointers are used to access. Some of these operations are rather bizarre, but they will add to your knowledge of pointers. Simply bear in mind throughout all discussions that a pointer "is a special variable that holds a memory address." That's all that it is.

Pointers to Structures

Structures in the C programming language provide a means of defining a single variable that is actually composed of a collection of many variables. Of course, arrays also provide a means of combining several variable storage areas into one accessed unit. However, the data types in a structure or a union do not have to be of the same type.

There are several different ways to create structures. The following method is the most common:

```
struct dbase {
        char client[30];
        int acctnum;
        double amount;
} ;
```

This example declares a structure named *dbase*. The structure is a collection of variables of different data types. The first `struct` element is named `client` and is a `char` array. The second and third are numeric types named `acctnum` and `amount`. This collection of variables may be accessed via the structure tag name, `dbase`. The following program shows one method of doing this:

```
main()
{

      struct dbase r;

      strcpy(r.client, "Jones, M.");
      r.acctnum = 12;
      r.amount = 23917.33;

      printf("%s\n%d\n%ld\n", r.client, r.acctnum, r.amount);

}
```

The expression:

```
struct dbase r;
```

defines a variable, `r`, which is a structure of type `dbase`. Within the body of the program, the structure member operator " `.` " connects the structure name (`r`) and the member name. Therefore, r.client accesses the structure element **client** and is used as the target argument to **strcpy()**. The int and double elements are assigned values, again using the structure member operator.

To display the contents of each structure element, **printf()** is invoked. Again the structure member operator comes into play with each of the arguments to this function.

Pointers to structures are very common in the C programming language, so common that a special operator is used for accessing structure elements by a pointer. The structure pointer operator -> is used to access a member of a structure using a pointer variable. The following program is a copy of the one above, except the structure elements are accessed via a pointer:

```
main()
{

    struct dbase r, *q;

    q = &r;

    strcpy(q -> client, "Jones, M.");

    q -> acctnum = 12;
    q -> amount = 23917.33;

    printf("%s\n%d\n%ld\n", q -> client, q -> acctnum, q -> amount);

}
```

In this program example, the declaration:

```
struct dbase r, *q;
```

names r a variable of type dbase and q a pointer of the same type. The next program line assigns q the address of r. Pointer q now points to the storage address reserved for struct dbase.

The structure pointer operator is used to access each structure element. This special operator is simply a convenient shorthand method of access when dealing with pointers. The expression:

```
q -> client
```

means exactly the same thing as:

```
(*q).client
```

The latter uses the structure member operator "." in conjunction with the unary * operator for access. The parentheses are necessary because the structure member operator "." takes higher precedence than does the unary * operator.

Pointers to structures are necessary when passing a whole structure to a function. C language passes arguments to functions by value, so it is necessary to pass the address of the structure to the function in order to gain access to the data elements. The following program shows how this may be done:

```
struct test {
        int a;
        char b;
        char name[20];
} ;

main()
{

        struct test r;

        load(&r);

        printf("%d  %c  %s\n", r.a, r.b, r.name);

}
void load(s)
struct test *s;
{

        s -> a = 14;
        s -> b = 'A';
        strcpy(s -> name, "Group");

}
```

A structure named `test` is defined with three elements of type `int`, `char`, and `char` array. Variable `r` is declared a variable of type `struct test`. The **load()** function is called and is passed the memory address of `r`. Within the function, `s` is declared a pointer of type `struct test`. This pointer has the address of the structure and uses the structure pointer operator to access each of the three structure elements. Since `s` is a pointer, assignments are made to the memory locations of each of the elements. These values are written directly to the structure, proper. On returning to the calling program, the values `14`, `A`, and `Group` will appear on the screen.

When dealing with structures, there is no problem with individual access of each element. However, when the structure as a whole is to be passed as an argument, a pointer to the structure is required. Pointers to structures have their own connective operators that allow for access in a convenient, shorthand manner. Trying to access a structure via a function call that does not include the structure address is an error and will result in garbage writes to and reads from the structure.

Pointers to Pointers

While not too much has been said about it, pointers have addresses too. I'm not referring to the addresses they are assigned, but the exclusive address of each pointer that is declared. In an earlier discussion on memory addressing, it was stated that small compiler models used 2-byte pointers, while large models used 4-byte pointers. This refers to the exclusive area set aside for each declared pointer to store an address assigned to it. This is confusing. We know that all standard variables have two values. The first is an address value or the place in memory where data is stored. The second is an object value or the data that is stored at the exclusive address.

What makes pointers a little more difficult to understand is that their object values *are* memory addresses. However, like all variables, pointers have two values as well. The first is the address value where storage is set aside for the pointer to store its object.

The second value is the object value, but in this case, the object is *another* address.

It's obvious that pointers must have a fixed address to store their objects. How else could data be stored except in memory? To further illustrate this point, observe the following program:

```
main()
{

      int *x;
      char *a;
      long *y;
      double *d;

      printf("%u  %u  %u  %u\n", &x, &a, &y, &d);

}
```

Here's our old friend, the unary **&** operator, which is used in front of standard variables to return their address values. Here, the same operator is used in front of pointer names to return their address values. Therefore (as unusual as it may sound), the expression:

```
&x
```

in the above example is a pointer to a pointer. This names the memory address pointer **x** uses to store the addresses of other objects. In most programming assignments, it is seldom necessary to access the exclusive address used by pointers, but the following program shows what is possible. This program example exercises the pointer-to-a-pointer concept using a rather roundabout method:

```
main()
{

      char *b, c[10];
      int x, *a;
```

```
        strcpy(c, "Goodbye");

        b = "HELLO";
        a = &b;
        x = &c[0];
        *a = x;

        printf("%s\n", b);

}
```

What does this program display on the screen when `b` is handed to **printf()**? `b` is a `char` pointer that is assigned the address of the constant `"HELLO"`. The correct answer is:

```
Goodbye
```

This is displayed when the object at the address in `b` is written to the screen by **print()**. How can this be? The answer is not easily explained, but I'll try.

First of all, we must look at **strcpy()**, which copies `"Goodbye"` to `c`, a char array. Next, `b` is assigned the address of `"HELLO"`, the constant value that you probably thought would be displayed by this program. However, the plot thickens! Pointer `a` is now assigned the address of pointer `b`, using the unary `&` operator to gain access to the exclusive storage area of the latter pointer. The expression `&b` is a pointer to a pointer. Now, `x`, an `int`-type standard variable, is assigned the address of the `char` array. No, `x` is not a pointer, but there's no law that says it can't be assigned a memory address, as long as that address is in the normal integer range. In this usage, `x` doesn't point to `c`, as a standard variable can't "point." The value stored by `x` also happens to be the same value as an address location, but this is not a pointer to that address. In other words, you cannot directly access array `c` via `x` . . . *but* you *can* access it *indirectly.*

The coup de grace is writing the address value that is contained in `x` to the memory location pointed to by pointer `a`. Remember, `a` has the address of the exclusive storage area for pointer b. This area has been invaded, violated, and changed to a new address, this being the address of array c, which points to the bytes containing "Goodbye". Notice that a was declared a pointer of type int. This means that *a = x writes the value in x to the address a points to as a 2-byte integer. Two bytes are assigned to pointers using the small-memory-model compiler option, so an int pointer is the logical type to use for changing the object address in any pointer.

All of this is "going around the barn" to simply assign b the address location of c. The easy way to have effected this operation would be to replace all of the code following:

```
b = "HELLO";
```

with:

```
b = c;
```

That's all the varied assignments and hidden manipulation did in the above program.

In fact, the ridiculous avenues traveled in this latest example are on a par with the contents of a char array being changed by a function that has been passed the address of the array. The only difference here is that the memory address *object* of b was being altered by a pointer that had b's memory address. To further aid you in understanding the previous program, it is presented again with comments:

```
main()
{

    char *b, c[40];
    int x, *a;

    strcpy(c, "Goodbye"); /* Copy constant into c */

    b = "HELLO";     /* assign b memory address of HELLO */
    a = &b;       /* read STORAGE address of b into a */
                  /* Note: a is an int pointer; b is a char */
```

```
    x = &c[0];  /* Variable x is assigned address VALUE */
                /* x is not a pointer. Its object value */
                /* is an integer that equals the address */
                /* of &c[0]. */
    *a = x; /* Write value in x as an int (2-bytes) to *a */
            /* *a accesses two bytes of memory as its */
            /* storage unit */

    printf("%s\n", b);  /* Display what b points to */

}
```

Declared Pointers to Pointers

The concept of a pointer having the exclusive storage address of another pointer is, perhaps, a bit exotic but is nothing to get alarmed about in C programming. In most applications, you don't see pointers to pointers very often, but they can and do occur.

The former program was an example of doing this within the framework of what had already been discussed previously. However, a pointer-to-a-pointer is a valid variable in C and is specially declared. The following program demonstrates this:

```
main()
{

        int x, *p, **ptp;

        x = 454;
        p = &x;
        ptp = &p;

        printf("%u  %d\n", *p, **p);

}
```

In this program `**ptp` is declared a pointer-to-a-pointer of type int. This means that ptp expects to be handed the address of a pointer. Variable x is assigned a value of 454; then its address is assigned to pointer p. Next, the address of pointer p is assigned to pointer-to-a-pointer ptp. The **print()** function is invoked to better illustrate the results. If you think of the pointer-to-a-pointer as:

```
*(*ptp)
```

it may be a little easier to comprehend. In any event, this program will display the memory address of pointer p and then the object value of 454. When dealing with pointers to pointers, we must keep track of the unary * operators. The expression:

```
**ptp
```

accesses the object of the pointer whose address the pointer-to-a-pointer has. However:

```
*ptp
```

returns the address assigned to the pointer-to-a-pointer. We can even become more bizarre and say that in this example:

```
&ptp
```

is a pointer-to-a-pointer-to-a-pointer.

The following program demonstrates the use of pointers to pointers of type char:

```
main()
{

        char a[20], *b, **c;

        strcpy(a, "Capacitor");

        b = a;
        c = b;

        printf(%s  %c\n", *c, **c);

}
```

This program will display:

```
Capacitor C
```

Remember, a pointer-to-a-pointer is a pointer within a pointer as well. The unary * operator is used to differentiate the objects being sought. If we think of c in this program as * (* c), then * c returns the address handed to c in the assignment line:

```
c = b;
```

and * * c accesses the ultimate object that the "pointer that is pointed to points to." That's quite a mouthful, but what we are faced with here is stacked pointers. Most programmers refer to these as "nested pointers," but thinking of them as stacked usually provides better comprehension. It is the object that is nested, and not the pointers. At the bottom of the heap in a pointer stack is the ultimate object. Above that object is a pointer that points to it. Above that pointer is a pointer-to-a-pointer. To get to the object, you have to start at the top with the pointer-to-a-pointer, go through the pointer, and finally access the object.

In the above program, * c is the memory address of the nested object, passed to the pointer-to-a-pointer by the pointer whose address it was assigned. The expression * * c is the object at the bottom of the stack. In order to display a string, the string address is handed to **printf()**. This is what * c is in the above program, while * * c is the 1-byte object at the same address that returns the first character in the string.

In C, we can create as high a stack of pointers as is desired. The following program reaches utterly ridiculous proportions:

```
main()
{

    int x, *p, **ptp, ***ptptp, ****ptptptp;

    x = 274;
    p = &x;
    ptp = &p;
```

```
        ptptp = &ptp;
        ptptptp = &ptptp;

        printf("%d\n", ****ptptptp);

}
```

As you might have guessed, this program displays the object value of 274 on the screen.

Understand that this is not a practical program. The chances of encountering such a monstrosity in a working program are very, very slim. However, this example does demonstrate the "deeply nested" capabilities of pointer operations, and it's good to understand the pointers-to-pointers principle in the event that an application arises that can make use of the concept.

Summary

Pointers to structures and to unions (closely aligned with a struct but utilizing only one memory location for storage, regardless of the number of elements) are absolutely essential when passing the structure to a function. Arguments to functions in C are passed by value, so the address of the structure must be handed to any function that is expected to effect operations on any of its elements. Pointers to structures are so common that a special structure pointer operator is available that allows for a type of shorthand notation when dealing with pointers to structures. Pointers to structures are essential for more elaborate database-type operations that involve creating linked lists and other complex organizations of data that can be accessed by a single variable.

Like all variables, pointers have two values. The one most frequently discussed is the right value or object value. However, a pointer's object value is an address. We normally think of the "lvalue" (left value) as being an address. A pointer also has an "lvalue" that is the address location of storage assigned exclusively to a pointer in order for it to store its object, which is the address of (presumably) another memory location.

When a pointer is declared to receive the "lvalue" or address of another pointer, then it is known as a "pointer-to-a-pointer." We can stack these pointers many layers high, although most applications do not take the nesting to the extent of some of the examples in this chapter.

While you probably will not find a pressing "need" to resort to pointers to pointers, it is important to understand the concept, so that this feature of the C programming language may be utilized when best programming efficiency and expression demand such operations.

Chapter 10

Source Code Format

The final chapter in this text may go unread, unnoticed, and unappreciated, but it contains information that can make the difference in understanding the C programming language and all of its many exotic, interesting, and powerful aspects. The most basic level of understanding any language begins with the examination of source code. How this source code is "presented" seems to be taken for granted by a growing number of C programmers, and this activity can create some very difficult problems.

When C language was first introduced, its source code was presented in a simple, easy-to-read format. The following program is an example:

```
main()
{

        int x;
        char a[40];

        strcpy(a, "Format");
```

```
          for (x = 0; x <= 10; ++x)
               printf("%s\n", a);

}
```

This program is very expressive, very easy to comprehend, because it is written in a style that "expresses" its intent. The **main()** function falls on the left-hand margin. The opening brace is on this same margin immediately below the function name. Then, there is a blank line, a separation.

Next, the declaration "block" appears, indented five spaces. All declarations are made in this block, which is then differentiated by another blank line.

The next block is also indented five spaces and is used for immediate assignments to variables. In this example, **strcpy()** is used to write the constant to array `a`. Another blank line serves to separate the initial assignment block from the next program operation.

A **for** loop is presented in the normal fashion. Its single object of control is a **printf()** function. Note that this line is indented five more spaces. The closing brace signaling termination of the execution run under control of **main()** is again on the left margin and separated by a blank line. The opening and closing braces encompassing the code under control of **main()** are easily identified because of their placement in relationship to other program statements.

While the expressiveness of C means many things, the presentation of the source code is a major part of this, to my way of thinking. Now, let's take the previous program and write it in the following manner:

```
main(){
int x;
char a[40];
strcpy(a,"Format");
for(x=0;x<=10;++x)
printf("%s\n",a);}
```

Is this program easy to understand? My immediate answer is "No!" It will compile and run exactly as the previous program did. The compiler sees no difference at all. As a matter of fact, this entire program could have been written to a continuous line with no difference in operation. However, the compiler sees things in one way, and we humans see them in another. The above example has no order, it has no expressiveness, and it is, possibly, an over-exaggeration of the way many people are writing C programs today.

I came to C programming from a BASIC language environment. One of the major problems with BASIC interpreters of the older genre lies in the impossibility of "easily" deciphering this language's source code. There was no order and no expression.

A major influence on the learning of the C programming language is the ability for the student to comprehend small portions of a complex program. At first, such a program may be extremely simple from the experienced programmer's point of view. However, the student is "working in the dark" in many areas that are known almost by instinct by the experienced programmer. The only solution is to have the student break each program down into blocks. If those blocks are not clearly delineated, the student's job is increased tenfold . . . or more.

Proper C language source code format calls for a space between numeric operators and their left and right values, as has been demonstrated throughout this entire text. Let's examine the following program as an example:

```
main()
{

        int h, i, *x, *y, z;

        i = 10;
        z = 20;

        x = &i;
        y = &z;

        h = *x * *y / ((float) *y / *x);

        printf("%d\n", h);

}
```

Again, this program is arranged according to good formatting principles. The assignment block has been broken down into three parts. The first assigns auto variables, the second assigns memory addresses to pointers, and the third assigns h the value of several mathematical operations on the previous variables. The block could have been written in one section without the blank-line separators, but, to me, this makes the program more understandable.

Now, let's take this same program and reformat it in the manner some programmers tend to use:

```
main()
{
int h,i,*x,*y,z;
i=10;
z=20;
x=&i;
y=&z;
h=*x**y/((float)*y/*x);
printf("%d\n",h);
}
```

What we have here is a hodgepodge. The program is so simple that it can be deciphered with a bit of study . . . if you know C language fairly well. If not, it may take longer. The point here is that the original program from which this poorly formatted copy was made is immediately comprehended. The operation of the previous program literally jumps out at anyone reading the source code who has even a minimal C background.

The whitespace between each character in the assignment and declaration lines "cleans up" the source code. The line:

```
h  =  *x**y/((float)*y/*x);
```

is almost frightening! How do we differentiate the multiplicative operator * from the unary * operator? Or is y in this example a pointer-to-a-pointer using two unary * operators? This program will execute in a normal manner, but the formatting of the source code is "garbage." GIGO (garbage in, garbage out) is a term coined to describe computer output based on erroneous input. The same applies to a human being. This type of confusing notation leads to problems of understanding. Maybe the student simply fails to comprehend anything about the program and gives up in disgust, or even worse, garners an incorrect impression of what is taking place and proceeds onward armed with this incorrect assumption. This leads to difficulties multiplied, and is one of the prime reasons why some programmers simply drop C language completely, averring that it is a ridiculous language with no form whatsoever.

Or take the following example, which is even worse:

```
main()
{
int h,i,*j,x,*y,**z;
x=14;
y=&x;
z=&y;
i=22;
j=&i;
h=*j***z/**z;
printf("%d\n",h);
}
```

The assignment line to h is a killer. What does it mean? If it had been written?

```
h = *j * **z / **z;
```

it still wouldn't be the easiest expression to decipher, but it would be far simpler.

In order to learn C, you must write your source code in a manner that allows for visual comprehension. A source code format has been established to provide the necessary clarity. It was not arrived at arbitrarily. I admit that when I first took up C language, having come from a BASIC interpreter environment, I did most of the awful things alluded to above. I also got nowhere on my first try. I was one of those programmers who gave up in disgust after my initial efforts. The second time around, I decided to do it like they did it in the book (K&R "The C Programming Language"). This was the most important thing I ever did for myself in regard to learning C, although I wasn't aware of it at the time.

When I devote an hour or so to teaching proper formatting while conducting a C language seminar, I get all kinds of resistance. "If it doesn't make any difference to the compiler as to how many white-spaces and blank lines there are in a program, why go to all the extra bother?" is what I often hear, especially from BASIC programmers who usually "hug" the left margin with all of their program lines. Or, "As long as I understand what I write, why use a format developed by someone else?"

These questions are legitimate ones, and they are asked out of ignorance, not laziness. The answer to both of these is that you have to be able to understand your own code, and you will *not* if you don't stick to an organized, symmetrical, expressive format! Sure, you can write a program today, and if it's not too complex, you will be able to comprehend what you wrote a week from now. But if it's complex, you may lose all track of what's taking place, not next week, but within the next *hour* of programming.

In 1984, I began work on CBREEZE, a translator program that accepts BASIC language source code and converts it to C source code. It does this without using hidden functions, and it does what it does for the student trying to learn C. To demonstrate the CBREEZE conversion output, consider the following BASIC source code:

```
10 FOR X%=0 to 4000
20 PRINT X%
30 NEXT
40 PRINT"now is the time for all good men"
50 Y%=21
60 PRINT Y%*23
```

This simple program is converted to its exact equivalent C language source code by CBREEZE, which outputs:

```
main()
{

        int x, y;

        for (x = 0; x <= 4000; ++x)
             printf(" %d \n", x);

        printf("now is the time for all good men\n");

        y = 21;

        printf(" %d \n", y * 23);

}
```

This C program has not been "touched by human hands." Maybe that's why it looks so clean! This is the exact output from CBREEZE, and it follows proper C language formatting to the letter. Now, if a program can do this, so can a human being, because it was a human who wrote the program in the first place.

This program is easy to understand and looks much better than:

```
main() { int x, y; for (x = 0; x <= 4000; ++x) printf(" %d \n",
x); printf("now is the time for all good men\n"); y = 21; printf("
%d \n", y * 23); }
```

which is how the compiler sees it.

At this point in a seminar, I'm usually asked if I followed these formatting conventions when writing CBREEZE over a 2-year period of time, inputting more than 100,000 lines of source code. The answer is demonstrated in the following partial source code listing, which amounts to approximately one-third of the total source code of one of the "smaller" modules in the CBREEZE translator:

```
/* Copyright (c) 1984 Robert J. Traister & Associates */
araysort (qw)
char *qw;
{

     struct vfile *fp, *fdd, *vopen();
     FILE *fd;
```

```
char a[250], b[260];
int x, d, z, xyz;

x = d = z = 0;
x = 0;

fp = vopen(qw, "r");
fdd = vopen("temp.ox", "w");

while ((vgets(a, 200, fp)) != NULL)
      if ((index(a, "DIM ")) >= 0)
            x = getout(a);

vwind(fp);

if ((fd = fopen("aray.xc", "r")) == NULL) {
      while ((vgets(a, 200, fp)) != NULL)
            vputs(a, fdd);

      vclose(fp);
      vclose(fdd);
      return;
}

while ((vgets(a, 200, fp)) != NULL) {
      while ((fgets(b, 250, fd)) != NULL) {
            replace(b, "\n", "");
            while ((z = index(a, b)) >= 0 && (isalpha(a[z - 1])) == 0)
                  scarp(a, z);
      }

      rewind(fd);

      vputs(a, fdd);

}

unlink("aray.xc");
vclose(fp);
fclose(fd);
vclose(fdd);

}
```

Again, this is a portion of one of the smaller modules in the

CBREEZE translator. This program took years to complete. Can you see how important proper formatting is? During the authoring of this software, I might have written one module in January and not referenced it again for 6 months. When it was time to return to this same module to make coding updates, it was often necessary to study what I had written 6 months ago in order to refresh my memory as to exactly what I had programmed and why! Can you imagine what agony I would have gone through had this module looked like the following example:

```
araysort(qw)
char *qw;
{
struct vfile *fp,*fdd,*vopen();
FILE *fd;
char a[250],b[260];
int x,d,z,xyz;
z=d=z=0;
x=0;
fp=vopen(qu, "r");
fdd=vopen("temp.ox","w");
while((vgets(a,200,fp))!=NULL)
if((index(a,"DIM "))>=0)
x=getout(a);
vwind(fp);
if((fd=fopen("aray.xc","r"))==NULL) {
while((vgets(a,200,fp))!=NULL)
vputs(a,fdd);
vclose(fp);
vclose(fdd);
return;
}
while((vgets(a,200,fp))!=NULL) {
while((fgets(b,250,fd))!=NULL) {
replace(b,"\n","");
while((z=index(a,b))>=0&&(isalpha(a[z-1]))==0)
scarp(a,z);
}
rewind(fd);
vputs(a,fdd);
}
```

```
unlink("aray.xc");
vclose(fp);
fclose(fd);
vclose(fd);
}
```

If I had programmed in this manner, CBREEZE would not be on the market today. It would never have been completed. If you have never been involved in a commercial software programming environment, then you can't know that "not understanding what you wrote yesterday" is an ongoing ordeal. The complexities and variations involved in one project demand methods of deciphering what may have been written at 3:00 in the morning after 20 hours of straight programming effort some months after the fact!

Again someone will ask "Why can't I develop my own formatting system, one that suits me best?" The first response is that you are probably not qualified to do so, which always elicits an evil look from the person asking the question. More important, it is mandatory in commercial programming environments that others on your team be able to read what you wrote. If you have your own formatting code, and 10 other team members have theirs, the system breaks down. You may not be working with a team now, but there is always that possibility in the future. Don't develop bad habits!

For me, the correct method of writing C source code, from the standpoint of formatting, has become automatic. I do not consider it a shortcut to, say, delete the spaces between operators and their left/right values. To purposely delete these spaces would take me far longer than to put them in, such is the "instinctive" formatting method that I have developed from thousands of hours at the keyboard.

You will grasp the concepts of C language pointers discussed in this text and every other phase of C language if you "make" yourself adhere to the programming conventions outlined here and garnered directly from "The C Programming Language" by Kernighan and Ritchie.

However, there are plenty of bad examples of C source code around to influence beginners. Unfortunately, many of these less than ideal examples appear in the documentation that accompanies some of the most popular compilers. The Turbo C manuals are relatively "clean," but there are occurrences of "poor" formatting in these texts that are being used by many beginners to learn C. "If the people who wrote the software do it this way, why shouldn't I?" is a legitimate question that I can only answer with "Don't do it because it's *wrong!*" Incidentally, I'm sure a number of programmers will not agree with my very strong opinions on formatting source code, while others will. I will state for the record that, as a C language teacher, I am more than a little concerned about the "bastardization" of what is a beautiful language format. The ANSI C standard was developed to provide standardization to the C programming language. This is good, and I believe we need to carry this standard forward to source code formatting as well. The reason for this is not to preserve the grand old heritage of C language, doing it the way those first C pioneers did. This should be done for clarity and understanding, allowing more programmers into the ranks.

As I was writing this text, a commercial software package arrived that I hoped to review for a magazine article. Believe it or not, the documentation was filled with source code examples that used left-margin tactics—that is, no indentations, no separators, no nothing! I sent it back!

Format for a Format

The following guidelines are those that were used by the CBREEZE translator as rules of format. Perhaps they will aid you in formatting your own C programs.

Braces

Braces ({ }) encompass a major control module. If that module is contained in a function, then the opening brace is positioned immediately under the function name and declaration sequence on the left margin as in:

```
char *strcpy(a, b)
char *a, *b;
{
```

Using the more modern style, this function fragment would read:

```
char *strcpy(char *a, char *b)
{
```

When braces are used to confine operational blocks within a program, such as would be the case with a loop containing more than one program statement, the opening brace follows the control expression on the same line and is separated by a single whitespace as in:

```
for (x = 0; x < 456; ++x){
     printf("%d\n", x);
     y += 5;
}
```

The closing brace is placed on the margin position that began the control expression and on a separate line immediately beneath the encapsulated statements.

Indentations

Indentations are always made in steps of 5. If we assume that **main()** is located on the left-hand margin (indent 0), then all other program statements are indented at locations 5, 10, 15, 20, etc. Assuming that the **for** loop example above begins at indent 5, then the statements within the loop are started at indent 10. Should there be a nested **for** loop within this one, then the **for** statement would be written at indent 10 and all program statements within this nested loop would be indented another five spaces (indent 15). The following program fragment shows this:

```
for (x = 0; x <= 465; ++x) {
     printf("%d\n", x);
     y += 5;
     for (z = 90; z > 0; --z) {
          strcpy(d, f);
          ++g;
     }
}
```

Note that the closing braces (}) are aligned under the block control elements they terminate. This makes nested operations easier to differentiate.

Parentheses

Parentheses (called "parens" in C jargon) immediately follow a function name, but are separated from **for, while,** and other statements by a space as is shown below:

```
for (x = 0; x < 5; ++x)
        strcpy(a, b);
```

The **for** statement is separated from the opening paren by a space, whereas the **strcopy()** function is immediately followed by the paren.

Arithmetic Operators

Arithmetic operators are delineated by a space on the left and on the right. Other types of operators usually are not. For instance:

```
i = x + y * z;
```

clearly shows the use of arithmetic operators as opposed to other operator types shown in the expression below, which also contains arithmetic operators:

```
i = x++ + ++y * *z;
```

Here, the increment operator (++) is not as readily confused with the addition operator (+), and the multiplicative operator (*) is not confused with the unary * operator.

Commas

Commas are always followed by a whitespace when used as argument delineators as in:

```
add(a, b, c, d, e);
```

The same applies to semicolons used within **for, do,** and **while** statements. Note that commas and semicolons are not preceded by a whitespace when used in this manner.

Summary

The proper formatting of a C program is essential in gaining a full understanding of the language. The difference between a properly and an improperly formatted program is like the difference between a neatly typed letter and one written in a messy scrawl.

By observing a few simple formatting rules, all source code will be easier to understand by you and by those who are interested in your programs. Of major importance is the fact that properly formatted programs will be more easily understood by the person who inputs the code lines, the programmer. This allows for quicker debugging of complex programs and facilitates the addition of changes that build from previously entered code.

Index